We Love to Sew

GIFTS

Fun Stuff for Kids to Stitch and Share

23 Projects

Annabel Wrigley

stitch your art out.

Publisher: Amy Marson

Creative Director: Gailen Runge

Art Director: Kristy Zacharias

Editor: Liz Aneloski

Technical Editors: Carolyn Aune and Gailen Runge

Cover/Book Designer: April Mostek

Production Coordinator: Jenny Davis

Production Editor: Joanna Burgarino

Illustrator: Kirstie L. Pettersen

Photo Assistant: Mary Peyton Peppo

Photography by Kristen Gardner, unless otherwise noted

Published by FunStitch Studio, an imprint of C&T Publishing, Inc., P.O. Box 1456, Lafayette, CA 94549

Library of Congress Cataloging-in-Publication Data

Wrigley, Annabel, 1972-

We love to sew : gifts : fun stuff for kids to stitch and share / Annabel Wrigley.

    pages cm

Audience: Ages 8-14.

ISBN 978-1-60705-997-4 (softcover)

  5658 5093 04/15

1. Textile crafts--Juvenile literature. 2. Gifts--Juvenile literature. I. Title.

TT699.W75 2015

746--dc23

         2014027292

Contents

Dedication/Acknowledgments   4

A Message from Rebecca Ringquist   5

6   Good to See You Again!

How to Use This Book   7

The Rules of Sewing   7

10   What Will I Need?

Basic Supplies   10

Choosing Your Fabrics   12

All About My Sewing Machine   14

The Parts of Your Sewing Machine   16

17   All the Skills You Need

Using Pins   17

Sewing Around a Corner   17

Making and Using Templates   18

Using an Iron   19

Using Paper-Backed Fusible Web   20

Making a Pom-Pom   21

Using a Hot Glue Gun   21

Sewing on a Button   22

Hand Sewing   23

27   Sewing Terms

30   The Beauty of Handmade

Projects

31   Gifts to Wear

Beautiful Bow-Tie Belt   32

Neat Men's Necktie   37

Pom-Pom Scarf   42

Stitchy Stripy Watchband   47

51   Gifts to Display

Patchy Sewn Mirror   52

Yo-Yo Garland   56

I Heart You Pillow   59

Family Tree Wallhanging   62

67   Gifts to Use

Oilcloth Tote with Fabric Handles   68

Super-Sweet-Smelling Lavender Sachets   74

Super-Cute Gadget Case   79

85   Gifts for Your Four-Legged Friends

Cozy Pet Bed   82

Squeaky Dog Bone   89

Embroidered Pet Portraits   92

Super Dog Collar   97

Kitty Catnip Toy   101

105   Gifts for Your School Friends

Felt Heart Paper-Clip Set   106

Covered-Button Pushpins   109

Scrappy Patchy Pencil Cup   112

Stitchy Coil Trinket Bowl   116

119   Let's Wrap It Up

Sewn Gift Bags   120

Paper Flower Gift Toppers   124

Felt Gift Card Holder   127

130   Patterns

134   Resources

135   About the Author

Acknowledgments

I never thought I would be given the opportunity to write another book. It is certainly a pinch-me experience to get to share my love of teaching children with all of you out there. I am forever grateful for your kind words and genuine enthusiasm for my little sewing world. Teaching children is the most fulfilling work for me, and I am forever grateful to be able to do it as my profession.

I would like to thank Darren, Ollie, and Ruby for their continued support and encouragement in my crazy writing and teaching schedule.

Thanks to everyone at C&T Publishing for all the kind words and hard work behind the scenes in putting this book together. Roxane, Liz, Kristy, Carolyn, and all the creative gang at C&T—I could not have done this without you!

I could never have done this without my amazing agent, Kate Mckean. You provide me with so much encouragement and support, and I am thankful for you every day!

Thanks to Kristen Gardner for, as always, helping me take this vision and make it into a beautifully photographed book. I am so lucky to have you as my creative co-pilot.

Finally, as always, my students are the reason I continue to write and teach and occasionally make music videos ... hmmm. You all inspire me to work harder every single day. Thank you!

Dedication

For my family

A Message from Rebecca Ringquist

When I was a kid, my dad made a living by designing and building furniture, and my mom made a living by designing and selling weavings. There was a woodshop in the basement, a weaving studio and shop on the main floor, and an apartment upstairs that we lived in. The store was open from Memorial Day to Labor Day, but the rest of the year it was just us three, home, making things. I often think about how lucky I was to grow up in the midst of so much making.

Oftentimes, my own childhood free time was spent fiddling with odds and ends in an effort to outfit my dollhouse to the nines. From salt clay I made cherry pies and tiny oranges, and from scraps of old clothes and toilet tissue I sewed tiny ramshackle quilts and pillows for the beds. Each time I made something new, I rearranged the house to accentuate it.

Now, as an adult with my own apartment, I still find myself itching for that same sort of satisfaction, and I often find myself rearranging furniture and shuffling stuff around. The things I treasure the most are the things that other people have made for me. The mint green pegboards my partner built hang in the brightest spot in our kitchen. On top of the dresser my dad built sits his tiny handmade model of our woodstove. My mom's handmade quilts and handwoven things sit on top of the piles of blankets. My grandma's paintings dot most rooms in our home quite prominently. I wouldn't trade those special gifts for anything, because the stories they remind me of are the most important ones I know.

Whether or not you're from a family of makers, you can choose to make things and give meaningful gifts. You can start a trend in your family. In a world of mass-produced objects, it's so nice to give someone something handmade that no one else could have made but you. Why not give something that will remind that special person of you and the time you took to make it for him or her? In the time it takes to shop for a gift, you could plan and make something wonderful to give to a friend, or your mom, or your grandma. When you walk into that person's room or home and see what you made displayed prominently—it's a great feeling!

I was so lucky last fall to meet my friend Annabel Wrigley, a kindred spirit when it comes to embracing the beauty of imperfection—a maker in the truest sense of the word. She approaches making things with a fierceness, an unwavering confidence, that never gets bogged down in what something "should" look like or how something "should" be made. Rather, she devises her own rules and patterns, finding fresh solutions to old problems.

The greatest gift of this book, a resource for kids who want to jump in without a lot of hoopla, is Annabel's permission to get started right away—her confidence that you can do it. Annabel asserts that with a bit of practice anyone can make something beautiful. This book of ideas, projects, and easy-to-follow photographs offers inspiration to make your family's gift giving easier, more original, and a whole lot more fun.

- Rebecca Ringquist

Good to See You Again!

Hey there! Welcome back.

It seems like only yesterday that I wrote my first "We Love to Sew" book. I am glad you have picked up this one and are feeling ready to make some super-fun and sweet things with me!

I was so excited to write this book all about gifts and gift giving! Don't you just love giving gifts? It truly is one of my favorite things in the world. I love making that something special for someone I love. There really is nothing better than the thrill of giving something that you have poured your heart and soul into making. Seeing the look of happiness on the face of the person who is given the gift, you know that that smile is all because of something that you made—yes, you! With your own two hands.

So let's get started and make gifts for every special person in your life. And don't worry—we won't forget your four-legged friends!

How to Use This Book

In this book, some of the projects are pretty easy, and some are a bit more challenging. You'll notice that each project has a symbol at the top. Here's what each symbol means.

easy peasy Start with these projects, especially if you are not super comfy yet with using your sewing machine. These are fun hand-sewing and craft projects that you'll have no trouble finishing.

a teeny bit more challenging You'll need a little confidence for these projects. You should be comfortable with using the sewing machine and hand sewing. You are going to have so much fun with these!

take your time and ask for help These projects need some patience and a great attitude. If you really know your way around your sewing machine, go for it! I know you can do it. You may want to ask for help from an adult or other experienced sewist. We all need a little help sometimes!

> **TIP**
> Practicing your skills on the easier projects in the book will help you gain confidence to tackle the more challenging ones!

The Rules of Sewing

I think it is so important for you to go into your sewing experience with a good knowledge of some do's and don'ts. I sure don't want to be telling you what to do, but there are some good things to know if you want to have a fun and successful sewing experience.

Keeping It Calm, Cool, and Collected

Yes, sewing is pretty fun and relaxing, but sometimes you may feel pressure to finish a project really fast or to speed up because you think it is important to always finish first. You may even feel pressure to sew better than someone else. You know what? In my classes, there is no pressure to be anything other than yourself. Be an individual, learn at your own pace, create your OWN work, and take pride in your individuality!

Express Yourself

Who says you can't put orange and purple together or mix a plaid with a polka dot? This is your project, and it is up to you to decide how wild and crazy or simple and sedate your project will be. Think about the person who will receive the gift and his or her personality and then go for it.

Slow Down!

It is amazing to me how many kids just want to finish a project as fast as possible. I think it is so important for you to start each new project with a deep breath and a whole lot of patience. You will love your work so much more if you just take the time to slow down—I promise!

Good to See You Again!

Practice, Practice, Practice

My best advice is to start with this easy practice exercise.

1. Start with a plain piece of fabric and use a ruler and an erasable pen to draw some straight lines on the fabric.

2. Thread your sewing machine with a bright-colored thread. Refer to your sewing machine manual if you need to.

Starting at the tippy top of the line, sew all the way to the bottom, working hard to keep your sewing on top of the line. You may start out a little wonky, but I pinky swear that after a few times you will feel more and more confident.

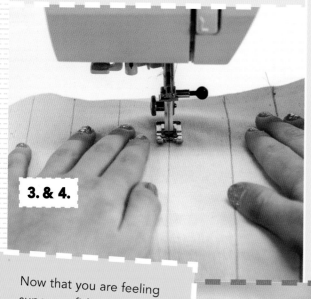

3. & 4.

After you have mastered this, turn over the fabric and line up the edge of the presser foot with the stitch line you made before and sew, keeping the presser foot right on the line. Go ahead and practice this on all the lines.

Now that you are feeling super confident, try drawing a big zigzag pattern on top of the fabric. Change your thread color and work on sewing the straight section and then pivoting at the zig (or is that the zag?).

1.

Stop at the turn.

2.

Turn the handwheel so that the needle is down.

3.

Lift the presser foot.

4.

Turn the fabric.

5.

Drop the presser foot and off you go!

Don't stop there! Try drawing some curves and other crazy patterns. At the end of this exercise, just iron to erase the pen marks and your fabric will look awesomely colorful and creative and will be begging to be used in a project (a bag could be cute!).

That was easy!

What Will I Need?

Each project has a whole list of supplies that are important for that particular project. There are a few things most of them have in common, and those are the basic supplies you will need!

Basic Supplies

SEWING MACHINE

Of course you will need a sewing machine for the majority of projects in this book, but do you know how to use one? Take the time to dig out the manual that came with your machine. If it has mysteriously disappeared, jump on the Internet. You will be amazed by how much valuable information you can find about your sewing machine!

SEWING MACHINE NEEDLES

Ever been to the store and been totally confused by the wall of sewing machine needles? Lucky for you that all our sewing machine projects only require the use of universal needles. Yay! Needle size 80/12 or 100/14 will work great for the fabrics we are sewing.

PINS

These are important to hold your work together for sewing. Straight pearl-head pins and flat plastic flower-head pins are my favorites. The longer length is perfect for our projects.

RULER

I always have a ton of clear quilting rulers hanging about! My most useful one is my clear 6½″ × 24″ quilter's ruler.

SCISSORS

A good sharp pair of scissors is super important, as I don't recommend the use of rotary cutters for kids. Make sure to have two pairs of scissors, one for fabric and one for paper. Paper cutting can really dull those fabric scissors!

SEAM RIPPER

Use this handy tool to remove that wonky stitch line. The sharp tip helps you cut stitching without putting a huge hole in your fabric.

HAND SEWING NEEDLES

Quite a few projects in this book require some hand sewing skills. Make sure you have some good sharp needles on hand.

EMBROIDERY NEEDLES

Embroidery needles are usually a little thicker and have a larger eye, making them easier to thread embroidery floss or perle cotton.

BUTTON THREAD

This is a nice thick and almost unbreakable thread that is handy to have around for attaching buttons and other sewing projects that involve heavier fabric.

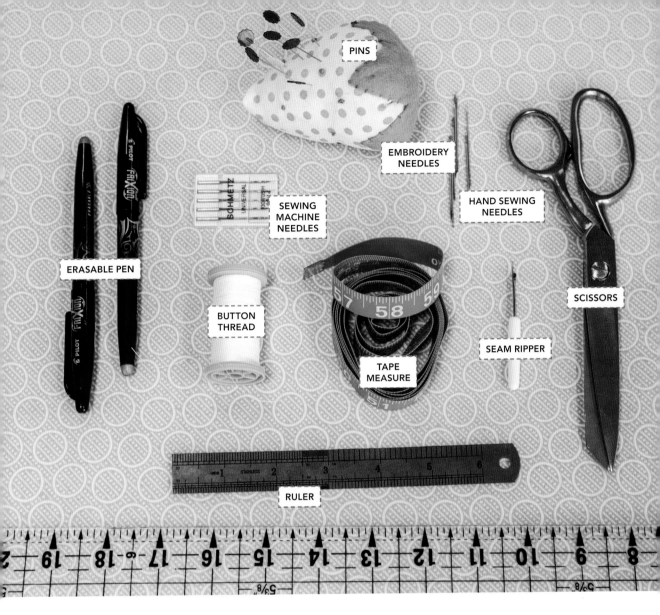

PINS

EMBROIDERY NEEDLES

HAND SEWING NEEDLES

SEWING MACHINE NEEDLES

ERASABLE PEN

BUTTON THREAD

TAPE MEASURE

SEAM RIPPER

SCISSORS

RULER

ERASABLE PEN

I always have half a dozen of these fantastic pens on hand for marking my fabric. You can write all over your work and then remove the marker with a hot iron. So cool! My faves are Pilot FriXion pens. You'll find them at an office supply store.

TAPE MEASURE

Sometimes you need to measure something super long, so a tape measure is really handy. It's also handy when you're measuring curves and things that are different shapes.

What Will I Need?

Choosing Your Fabrics

Choosing fabric is the most fun part of embarking on a new project. Your fabric choice can really help you create an individual and creative project that will be sure to wow everyone.

There are so many places to find fun fabrics. Fabric stores always have the very best selection, but you would be surprised how many fabrics you can find just lying around the house. Old clothes and thrift shop finds can provide a ton of fun fabrics for these projects. I just love the look of vintage floral sheets reused in fun projects!

Cotton

Cotton is the main fabric that we will be using in most of our projects in this book. Cotton is a great weight, is easily washable, and comes in a zillion different prints. I really love to work with quilting cotton. Some of the projects in this book require a heavier cotton fabric like cotton canvas or decorator-weight cotton. I like to use the heavier fabric for bags and pillows; it helps a project hold its shape a little better.

Felt

Felt is just about the best fabric to work with. It comes in tons of lovely colors, and the best part is that it doesn't fray. You can make the cutest flowers and shapes from it!

I love to use wool felt, but you can use any kind of felt you can find in the arts and crafts store.

TIP

Turn the iron down if you are ironing synthetic felt. It is made from plastic bottles, which means it will melt if the iron is too hot. It sometimes helps to lay a piece of fabric over the felt to protect it from the hot iron.

Cotton Canvas

I always have a huge bolt of cotton canvas on hand at the studio. It is the perfect fabric to practice sewing on. It is also perfect to line bags, to paint on, and to print on. It is usually pretty inexpensive and is great to have on hand!

All About My Sewing Machine

Sewing on a machine may seem a little ominous or scary; it is a piece of machinery, after all. I am here to tell you that with a little practice, you will be sewing like a pro. It's kind of like driving a car; you need to be able to control the speed and sew in a straight line! Pull out the manual and settle in for a good read. Your manual will explain all about the dials and stitches on your machine—how fun!

TIP

Not sure you'll remember all the bits and pieces on your machine? Grab a piece of decal paper and make your own homemade stickers for your machine. Stick one at each of the threading points to remind you how to thread the machine. When you feel confident about how to use your machine, you can remove the stickers without too much trouble.

WE LOVE TO SEW...GIFTS

Threading the Sewing Machine

Most modern machines are threaded in a similar way, usually from right to left. However, if you have an older machine, the threading may be completely different. This is a good time to check the manual.

Believe it or not, if one little section of your machine is not threaded correctly, it will make your thread into a knotted crazy mess. Take the time to really practice threading. You will be glad you did!

Sewing Machine Needles

Always make sure that you are fully stocked with universal sewing machine needles. Sometimes your sewing machine needle will break! You may accidently run over a pin or sew through something a little thick for your machine. There is nothing worse than running out of sewing machine needles when you are in the middle of a project.

To change the needle, loosen the little screw right beside the needle. You usually won't need a screwdriver for this. Remove the old needle and replace it with a new one. Tighten the screw so it is super-duper tight.

15

The Parts of Your Sewing Machine

We use simple sewing machines in the Little Pincushion classroom. Your machine at home may look similar. You are probably pretty familiar with most of the parts already, but I thought I would explain each one to you.

Tension control
This is really important. This dial controls the tension or tightness of the top thread. Usually if your stitching looks a little strange, it is because of the tension. Look at your manual or ask an adult for help if you are confused.

Stitch length selector
This is the dial you turn to choose how long your stitch length will be. A stitch length of 2.5 is a good standard setting for your machine. Your machine may have a different number or dial; play around with it to find a good even-sized stitch, not too big and not too small. Sometimes there is just a dial with different stitch lengths to choose from. You should turn it to a medium-sized stitch.

Handwheel
This round wheel at the end of the machine is the way to manually lift the needle up and down.

Thread take-up lever
This part of the machine helps you keep the correct thread tension as you sew. If your machine is not sewing properly or makes a loud thumping sound, it may be because the thread has become unthreaded from the take-up lever.

Presser foot lifter
This lever on your machine is in control of lifting and lowering the presser foot. Make sure to always have the presser foot down for sewing.

Feed dogs
These are like little hands that push the fabric under the presser foot. They keep the fabric moving without you having to push or pull it.

Presser feet
Most sewing machines come with a selection of presser feet to be used for all different sewing projects. In this book we will be using a regular sewing foot. We sometimes call the presser foot a chicken foot. It kind of looks like one, don't you think?

Reverse button
This is the little button you will need to press or push down to make the machine sew backward. Remember that whenever you start sewing, you should backstitch at the beginning and end.

All the Skills You Need

You will notice that at the beginning of most of these projects, there is a little section called "Special Skills." These are skills that you may not have yet, such as using a hot glue gun, using an iron, or using pattern pieces. This is a good time to ask a grown-up for a little help!

Using Pins

It is super important to know how to use pins correctly. Pins are a really big part of making your project look neat and even. Pins hold two (or more) pieces of fabric together so that they don't move when you sew.

My favorite way to pin is with the pins perpendicular to the edge of the fabric. I prefer it this way because the pins are easier to remove as I sew along!

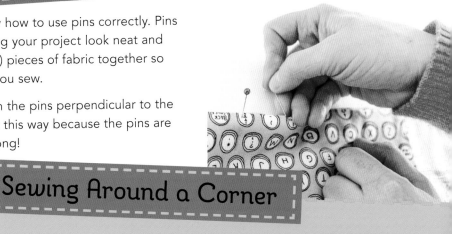

Sewing Around a Corner

Most projects in this book will require you to sew around a corner at some point. It is important to learn how to do this correctly so that your corners always look nice and neat!

1. Sew down the side of your work and stop approximately a presser foot's width from the corner.

2. Turn the handwheel so that your needle is down in the fabric.

3. Lift the presser foot and turn the fabric so that the presser foot is facing in the correct direction to sew the next edge.

4. Make sure that you do this for all your corners. I promise it will make your work look super awesome!

All the Skills You Need

Making and Using Templates

Some of the projects in this book have patterns that you will need to trace to make templates. The project instructions will tell you where in the book to find the patterns.

All the pattern pieces are just the right size for you to trace and use. Some of them may need to be joined together with tape, as they are a little large to fit on one page.

I love to copy my pattern pieces by tracing on tracing paper or parchment paper. You could even use white paper from your home printer. Tracing paper can be found at any arts and crafts store. If you don't already have parchment paper in your kitchen, you will find it in the grocery store near the aluminum foil. If your paper isn't big enough, tape a few pieces together to make a larger piece.

1.

Lay the paper over the pattern piece and trace the shape with a pencil. Make sure to add all the markings, like the no-sew zone and other placement marks.

2.

Cut out the shape with scissors.

3.

Pin the tracing-paper pattern shape to fabric and cut around it.

You could also trace around the shape with erasable marker and then cut it out!

Using an Iron

Ironing your project is the perfect way to make it look polished and finished. There is nothing worse than a wrinkled project after all that hard work you put in sewing.

1. Make sure that you ask an adult to supervise when you iron for the first time. Be sure to keep your body and your fingers out of the way when you are ironing.

2. Pay special attention to the fabric you are using. You will see that the iron has different settings for different fabrics. An iron on a hot cotton setting will melt a synthetic fabric.

As long as you pay attention to the settings, you should have no problem.

Sometimes steam can cause a nasty burn, so I like to turn off the steam and keep a little water spray bottle close by; I spray water on the fabric before ironing for a nice and super-smooth look. Most irons have a button to push to turn off the steam. Ask a grown-up to show you. All irons are a little bit different!

Using Paper-Backed Fusible Web

Fusible web is a wonderful product to use when you need to attach one fabric to another without having to pin. It is great for holding felt and fabric shapes in place until you are able to sew. I use paper-backed fusible web all the time. HeatnBond Lite is my all-time favorite. It lets you sew without gumming up your needle.

1. & 2.

Trace or draw the shape you need on the paper side of the fusible web.

Turn off the steam on your iron.

3.

Place the bumpy, fusible side down on the wrong side of the fabric and iron.

4.

When the fabric has cooled, cut out the shape.

5.

Peel off the backing paper.

6.

Position the shape on the fabric and iron it in place.

7.

Sew nice and neatly around the shape. Use an erasable pen to draw a stitch line if you need to.

Making a Pom-Pom

2. & 3.

Carefully slide the yarn off your hand, keeping the yarn together in a neat bundle.

Cut another piece of yarn and tie it around the middle of the yarn bundle. Make sure that the loops are free for trimming.

1.

Wrap yarn around the widest part of your hand about 75 times (or more for a bigger pom).

4. & 5.

Tie it super tight in a double knot.

Snip the loops with a sharp pair of scissors.

6.

Give the pom-pom an allover haircut until it is the size that you like.

Using a Hot Glue Gun

Hot glue guns are so awesome! But, yes, they are pretty darn hot. Always make sure you are using a low-temp glue gun. They usually have it written on the package at the store.

Always ask an adult before you use one and make sure to have a little bowl of ice water on hand in case of a burn.

Sewing on a Button

After years of teaching kids just like you, I am always surprised how many of them are afraid of sewing on a button. It is really super simple and can make your project look extra awesome! Have you seen how many amazing buttons there are out there? I have been collecting pretty ones for years.

1.

Mark the spot for your button.

2.

Thread a needle with button thread or embroidery floss. Tie a knot in the end of the thread.

3.

Hold the button on the fabric at the spot where you marked. Bring the needle up from behind the fabric and through a hole in the button.

4.

Pull the needle all the way through the hole and then push the needle down to the back of the fabric through the hole beside the one you just came through.

5. & 6.

Bring the needle back up from behind the fabric and through the hole and then down again just like before.

Repeat this a couple more times until the button feels tight and secure.

7.

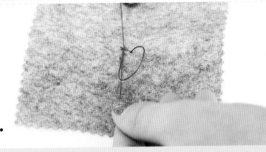

8.

Bring the needle up from behind the fabric but do not push it through the buttonhole. Instead, push it between the fabric and button and wrap the thread around underneath the button 3 or 4 times. This helps your button to be secure!

Push the needle back down to the back of the fabric and secure it with a double knot.

Trim the thread.

Hand Sewing

Hand sewing is the perfect technique to make your machine-sewn project look even better and craftier. It's easy to get used to working on only a sewing machine, and the less time you spend on hand sewing, the more challenging it will seem. Here's the great news: it's really, really easy and fun!

Our projects will require only a few kinds of hand stitches.

Sewing a Running Stitch

Running stitch is probably the simplest hand stitch. It is basically just an up-and-down stitch.

1.

Knot the end of the thread.

2.

Push the needle up from underneath the fabric.

3.

Push the needle down approximately ¼″ away from where you brought it up. Refer to the tip (page 24) to make it easier to sew even stitches.

4.

5.

Bring the needle up again another ¼" away and then push it down again, keeping your stitches as even as possible.

Continue sewing like this all the way around your project.

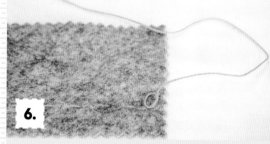

6.

TIP

It can be really helpful to use an erasable pen and draw dots on your fabric ¼" apart to use as a stitch guide. These dots can help you keep your stitches neat and even and can be removed with a hot iron.

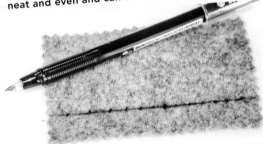

When you get to the end, make sure your final stitch ends on the back of the fabric. Tie a knot in the thread nice and close to the fabric.

Sewing a Whipstitch

Whipstitch is an easy stitch that is used to close holes on things like pillows and soft toys.

1.

2.

3. & 4.

Push the needle through both sides of the fabric opening and tie a double knot in the thread.

Bring the needle up through one side and out the other side of the fabric.

Move a little below and push the needle through both sides of the opening. Pull the stitch nice and tight so that the sides of the opening come together.

Don't forget to tie a knot when you are finished.

Sewing a Backstitch

I love to use backstitch with embroidery floss or perle cotton when I am embroidering letters or words. It makes a pretty, continuous line that looks good even around curves.

1. Bring the needle up from behind the fabric.

2. Push it down again at the next dot.

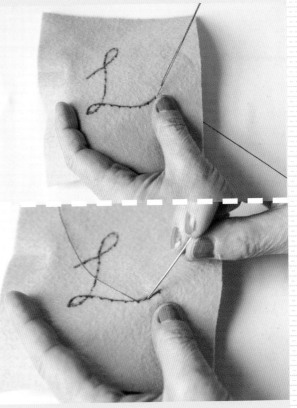

3.

Instead of continuing like a running stitch and sewing the stitch forward, you will bring the needle up ¼" away and then push it back down in the hole of the last stitch you made.

So basically you move forward and then stitch backward. It makes a nice continuous line without the spaces of a running stitch.

4.

Sewing a Vicki Knot

There is a traditional embroidery stitch known as the French knot. I have always found it a little tricky to teach to children. Lucky for me, my friend Vicki taught me her own variation, known as the Vicki knot. I am excited to share it with you!

1. Knot the end of an arm's-length piece of embroidery floss or perle cotton.

Note: An arm's length of thread is measured from your fingertips to your shoulder. This makes the thread piece easy to manage.

2.

3.

Thread the embroidery needle and bring the needle through the fabric from behind on a marked spot.

Tie a knot in your thread, but before you tighten the knot, place the tip of your needle in the center of the knot.

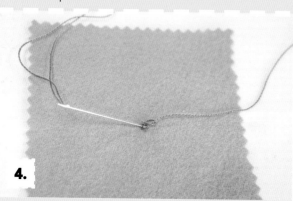

4.

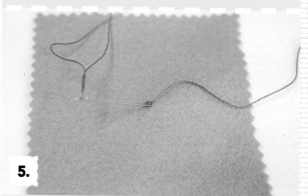

5.

Ease the knot down the needle until it is right on top of the fabric.

Tighten the knot.

6. Push the needle through to the back of the fabric and secure with a knot.

7. If you want a larger knot, tie a second knot in Steps 3–5 and treat both knots as one in Step 6.

Sewing Terms

There may be some words in these projects that you have never heard before. Never fear. I am here to explain them all to you!

LEAVE A TAIL

One of the most annoying things that happens to my students in class is when the sewing machine repeatedly becomes unthreaded. It takes time to have to constantly rethread your machine when all you really want to do is sew, sew, sew! I have an easy tip so that does not happen to you. Pull out an 8″-long "tail" of machine and bobbin thread before you begin sewing. That way, when the machine needle goes down, it won't take your thread with it.

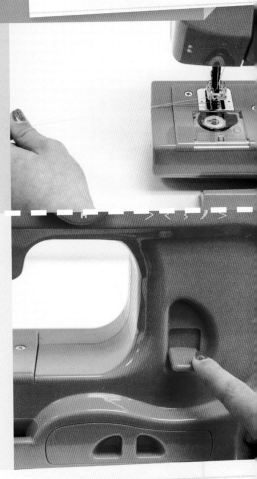

BACKSTITCH

It is important to backstitch at the beginning and end of every stitch line. Backstitching just creates a strong beginning and ending that prevents your stitching from coming undone. Most machines have a reverse button or lever that you will need to hold down to go backward. Take a look at your machine manual to find it.

When you start sewing a seam, sew a few stitches forward and then hold down the reverse button for a few stitches. Now let go of the button and continue forward until the end of the seam. When you get to the end of the seam, hold down the reverse button again to secure the stitches.

EDGE OF THE PRESSER FOOT ON THE EDGE OF THE FABRIC

Many sewing machines come with a regular presser foot that is ⅜″ from the center to the edge. For that reason, these projects use a ⅜″ seam allowance. That means that most of the projects can simply be sewn with the edge of the foot on the edge of the fabric!

27

FAT QUARTER

A fat quarter is a quarter of a yard, but it is not a regular quarter-yard, which is 9″ × 44″; it has a different shape. In order to get a fat quarter of fabric, you would divide one yard of quilting fabric into four large rectangles, so each rectangle measures 18″ × 22″.

Fat quarters are great because you can actually get more out of this measurement than with a regular quarter-yard. If you go to your local fabric store, you can usually find stacks of fat quarters by the shelves of quilt fabric. What's great is that they are inexpensive and a great way to add fabric variety to your projects!

RIGHT SIDES TOGETHER

It is important to sew with right sides together. This means that you match up the fabrics with the pretty (right) sides facing each other, and you sew on the wrong side. That way, when you turn your project right side out, there will be no messy raw edges showing.

Wrong side

Right side

NO-SEW ZONE

You may come across the term "no-sew zone" in this book. This is my own made-up term for the area where you don't sew … you know, when you are sewing a piece that needs to have an opening so it can be turned right side out.

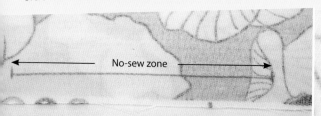

No-sew zone

SEAM

This is the stitching line you have sewn to join one piece of fabric to another piece of fabric.

WE LOVE TO SEW · GIFTS

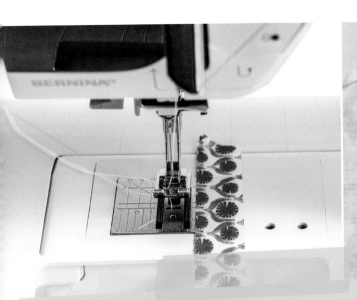

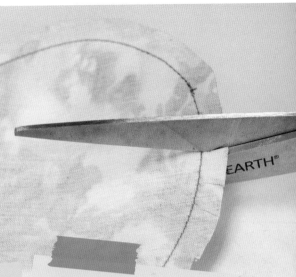

SEAM ALLOWANCE

This is the measurement from the edge of the fabric to the stitch line. The seam allowance for most of the projects in this book is ⅜″. If your presser foot only measures ¼″, you could use a piece of washi or masking tape as a guide. Place the inner edge of the tape ⅜″ out from the machine's needle. Sew with the edge of the fabric on the edge of the masking tape. I think it really helps when you have some way to line everything up.

CLIP THE CURVES

Sometimes when you are sewing something that has curves and needs to be turned right side out, you need to clip the curves so that the curves stay nice and curvy.

When you have finished sewing a curvy seam, use a sharp pair of scissors to carefully clip the fabric every inch. Make sure not to clip the stitching!

Do You Feel Confident?

So, now you are ready to set off and start sewing some of the projects from this book for all your family, friends, and pets!

→ **Threading your machine and bobbin?**

→ **Sewing with the edge of the presser foot on the edge of the fabric?**

→ **Sewing a straight line?**

→ **Pivoting around corners?**

→ **Using pins correctly?**

If you answered "No" to any of these questions, go back to the previous sections in the book and take a little more time. Ask for help!

The Beauty of Handmade

When I think of a handmade gift, I think of all the love that someone has poured into making that gift for me. That person actually sat down and thought about something that I would love and then set about making it … with his or her own two hands! How great is that? Often it is those thoughtful gifts that are my most favorite and treasured, whether it is a tiny feather in a matchbox or a scarf with all the trimmings.

Sometimes I think we just spend way too long sitting indoors, mesmerized by the TV or one of our many gadgets. It's pretty easy to get lost in a fun video game or an awesome movie. But I guarantee you will enjoy the process of making something with your hands so much more than using your hands to text or hold a game controller. Give it a try!

This process is made even more enjoyable when we are making something for someone else. I know that these are the gifts I treasure, the ones that have the most meaning.

Handmade gifts are the perfect way to tell someone how much you love him or her. (They are pretty good for the environment too!)

Don't worry—this book is not just about gifts for others. You can make a few gifts for your-self too. I know you'll want to!

Gifts to Wear

Beautiful Bow-Tie Belt

What Do I Need?

- ⅜ yard of fun fabric

- ½ yard of featherweight fusible interfacing

- 2 D-rings (1″)

- Fun-colored sewing thread to coordinate with the fabric

- Basic sewing supplies (page 10)

special skills

- Refer to The Rules of Sewing (page 7)

- Using an iron (page 19)

If you are using a ¼″ presser foot, don't forget to use washi tape as a guide to make the correct seam allowance width for this project (page 29).

Prepare the Pieces

1. Cut 1 piece of fabric and 1 piece of interfacing to measure 6″ × 10″ for the bow tie.

2. Cut 1 piece of fabric and 1 piece of interfacing to measure 3″ × 3½″ for the center piece of the bow tie.

3. Cut 1 piece of fabric and 1 piece of interfacing to measure 5″ wide and your waist measurement plus 8″ in length for the belt.

TIP

A good way to measure the length you need for the waist is to put on your favorite pants and run the tape measure through the belt loops (or at the belt line if the pants have no loops). Check the measurement on the tape and use that as your waist measurement.

Note: Most interfacing is only 20″ wide. For the long belt piece, you can cut 2 strips across the width of the interfacing and lay them end-to-end on the wrong side of the fabric.

Let's Make It

THE BOW TIE

1.

Iron the interfacing to the wrong side of the bow-tie pieces.

And you thought bow ties were just for the fellas! This sweet bow-tie belt is just crying out to be made in a million different colors and patterns for all your fashion-forward friends!

2. & 3.

Fold the 6″ × 10″ bow-tie piece in half lengthwise, right sides together, and pin along the long side.

Sew with the edge of the foot on the edge of the fabric.

4.

Turn the piece right side out, placing the seam in the center of the underside of the fabric piece. Press with an iron.

5. & 6.

Fold the fabric piece in half lengthwise with the seam sides facing out and pin along the short end.

Sew across the end with the edge of the presser foot on the edge of the fabric.

7.

Turn right side out and place the sewn seam on the center of the underside of the loop you have just sewn. Press with an iron.

8. & 9.

Fold the 3″ × 3½″ piece of fabric in half lengthwise with right sides together and pin along the long side.

Sew the pinned side with the edge of the foot on the edge of the fabric.

10.

Turn the piece right side out, placing the seam in the center of the underside of the fabric piece. Press with an iron.

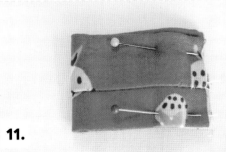

11.

Fold the piece in half, right sides together, matching the short ends. Pin in place.

12. & 13.

Sew down the pinned side with the edge of the foot on the edge of the fabric.

Turn this piece right side out and make sure that the seam is once again in the center of the underside. Press with the iron.

THE BELT

1.

Iron the interfacing to the belt piece.

2.

Fold in each short end ½″ and press with an iron.

3.

Fold the entire piece in half lengthwise with wrong sides together and press with an iron.

4.

Open out the strip so you can see the crease. Fold in a long edge to meet the crease and press with an iron. Then repeat with the other long edge.

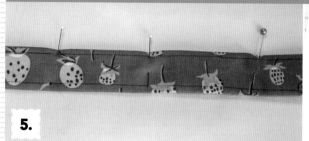

5.

Refold the piece on the crease so both long raw edges are on the inside. Press well with an iron. Make sure to use a few pins to hold the fold in place!

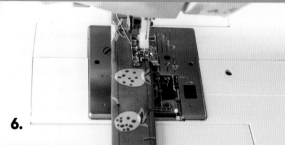

6.

Sew around the whole strip, sewing nice and close to the edge. It is sometimes easier to draw a line with an erasable marker for this!

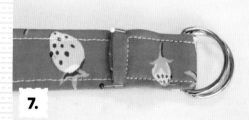

7.

Slide the 2 D-rings onto the end of the belt strip. Fold the belt end over 1½″, with the D-rings inside the fold. Pin the fold in place.

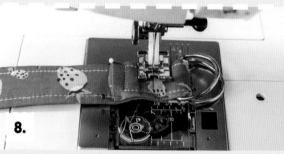

8.

Draw a stitching line about ½″ from the belt end. Draw another line about ½″ from the D-rings. Sew on the stitching lines to secure the D-rings and the folded end.

Finish Up!

Yay! Now you are ready to box up that sweet bow-tie belt and give it to your bestie!

1.

Slide the center bow piece along the belt until it is 3″ or 4″ from the rings.

2.

Slide the bow piece through the center bow piece. It helps to fold the bow tie in on both sides to make it a little easier. Open out the bow.

Neat Men's Necktie

What Do I Need?

- Old necktie (Thrift shops usually have a huge supply for a dollar or so.)

- 1¼ yards of fabric OR a piece of fabric measuring 20″ × 39″; you should cut your fabric so that the tie pattern is running parallel to the selvage (Since you can make 2 ties from the 1¼ yards, you could share the fabric with a friend.)

- 10″ × 10″ piece of a contrasting fabric

- Coordinating sewing thread

- Basic sewing supplies (page 10)

special skills

- Refer to The Rules of Sewing (page 7)
- Using an iron (page 19)

Prepare the Pieces

1. Using your seam ripper, carefully unpick the entire tie, starting at the back seam.

37

Thinking of a neat gift for Dad? I don't think you can beat a super-smart-looking necktie made by you! Pick a cute yet manly fabric and craft the perfect gift for your pop.

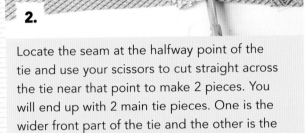

2.

Locate the seam at the halfway point of the tie and use your scissors to cut straight across the tie near that point to make 2 pieces. You will end up with 2 main tie pieces. One is the wider front part of the tie and the other is the narrower "tail" that will be behind the front part when the tie is tied.

3.

Press them with an iron, so they are nice and flat. These pieces will act as your pattern pieces.

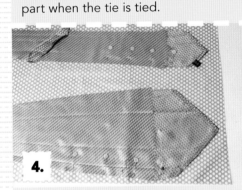

4.

Lay a single layer of fabric right side up on a flat surface. Pin the tie pieces to your fabric. Make sure to pin them with the right side of the tie piece facing up.

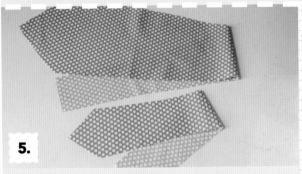

5.

Carefully cut out the pieces.

Let's Make It

1.

Place the 2 pieces right sides together and pin them as seen in the picture. Make sure the pieces are positioned exactly as shown in the photo. We are joining them together to make 1 long tie piece.

If you are using a ¼" presser foot, don't forget to use washi tape as a guide to make the correct seam allowance width for this project (page 29).

2.

Sew the pieces together with the edge of the presser foot on the edge of the fabric.

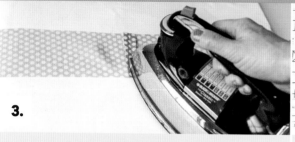

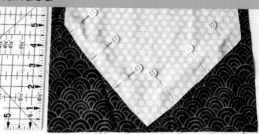

3.

Open out the seam and press it flat. Trim off any overhanging fabric from the edges.

4.

Lay the contrasting fabric faceup on a flat surface. Place the large tie end facedown on top of the fabric, so the contrasting fabric covers the bottom up to approximately 6½˝. Pin the contrasting fabric piece to the end of the tie, with the right sides facing. Pin the 2 sides of the point.

5.

Sew down around the points with the edge of the presser foot on the edge of the fabric.

TIP

When you are sewing around a corner like this, it is important to pivot correctly by putting the needle down in the fabric, lifting the presser foot, and turning the fabric.

6.

Carefully cut around the contrasting fabric.

7.

Cut the tip of the point of the fabric. Be careful not to cut the stitching. This helps the point be a little pointier when it is turned right side out.

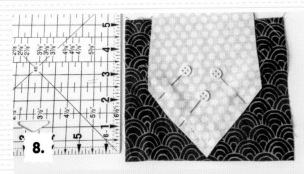

8.

Repeat Steps 4–7 with the other end of the tie, except this time you only need to measure up 5″ on the contrasting fabric.

9.

Turn the tie ends right side out and give them a good press with an iron.

10.

Fold the tie in half lengthwise, lining up the raw edges with right sides together, and pin.

11.

Sew all the way down the length of the tie, with the edge of the foot on the edge of the fabric, backstitching at both ends. Make sure not to sew around the point.

Finish Up!

1.

Turn the tie right side out.

2.

Iron so the seam is on the back of the tie!

Pom-Pom Scarf

Finished Size: Approximately 7¼″ × 49¼″

What Do I Need?

- ½ yard of lovely fleece or wool fabric (at least 50″ wide)
- 3 balls of yarn in fun colors
- Coordinating sewing thread
- 4 pieces of cardboard 5″ × 5″ (You can cut up a cardboard box.)
- Basic sewing supplies (page 10)

If you are using a ¼″ presser foot, don't forget to use washi tape as a guide to make the correct seam allowance width for this project (page 29).

special skills

- Refer to The Rules of Sewing (page 7)
- Sewing a whipstitch (page 24)
- Sewing around a corner (page 17)

Prepare the Pieces

Cut 2 pieces of scarf fabric to measure 8″ × 50″.

Let's Make It

THE SCARF

1.

Place the 2 scarf pieces right sides together and pin all the way around.

◄——— No-sew zone ———►

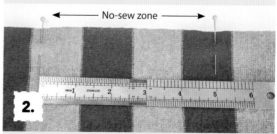

2.

Mark a 5″-long no-sew zone (page 28) near the center of a long edge of the scarf. This is the area that we do not want to sew.

Beat the chilly breeze with this soft and warm neck scarf. Make it your own with some bright and groovy pom-poms. This is so easy to sew that you will be making them for everyone on your birthday list! Pomtastic!

3.

Sew all the way around with the edge of the presser foot on the edge of the fabric. Be sure to leave the no-sew zone open.

4.

Trim the corners just outside the seamline. Don't snip the stitching!

5.

Turn the scarf right side out and iron it nice and flat.

6.

Pin the hole closed, making sure that you have folded the raw edges in, so everything stays nice and neat.

Use a whipstitch to sew the hole closed.

7.

THE MULTICOLORED POM-POMS

Slit — ——— Slit

1.

2.

Cut anchor slits in the middle of opposite edges of each piece of cardboard. Cut toward the center, but be sure not to cut all the way through. You want an inch or so in between the slits.

Place the end of the yarn in an anchor slit and wrap the first yarn color around the cardboard (50 times for thinner yarn or 30 times for fatter yarn).

Wrap the second color (75 times for thinner or 50 times for fatter).

Note: Each time you wrap a new color, make sure that it completely covers the last area of wrapping and each layer can spread out about 1″ past the previous layer.

3.

4.

5.

Wrap the third color (50 times for thinner or 30 times for fatter).

Cut a 10″ piece of yarn and wrap it through the slits and around the yarn bundle and tie a double knot.

6.

Tear away the cardboard carefully.

7.

Tie another yarn knot on top of the previous knot, except this time try to tie it even tighter. It may help to have a friend's finger hold down the knot!

8.

Use small sharp scissors to cut through the pom-pom loops.

9. & 10.

Give the pom-pom a haircut by evenly trimming the pom-pom down.

Use the other cardboard pieces and repeat Steps 2–9 to make a total of 4 pom-poms.

Sew a pom-pom to each corner of the scarf with button thread. Make sure to pass the needle through the center of the pom-pom a few times and then finish off with a knot.

11.

Stitchy Stripy Watchband

What Do I Need?

- An old watch face with a watchband bar or a watch face from a craft store (I used a watch face with a 1″ bar. The watch bar is the little bar on each side of the watch face where a strap is normally attached. Use a tape measure or ruler to measure the length of the bar; that will help you decide how wide your fabric should be.)

- 4″ × 22″ strip of fun fabric

- 4″ × 22″ strip of featherweight fusible interfacing

- Fun-colored thread to coordinate with the fabric

- Snap kit (which includes a snap tool and size 15 or 16 snaps)

- Hammer (to use with the snap tool)

- Basic sewing supplies (page 10)

special skills

- Refer to The Rules of Sewing (page 7)
- Using an iron (page 19)

Prepare the Pieces

1. Measure your wrist by wrapping the measuring tape around your wrist twice. The watchband will be super long, so you can wrap it around your wrist twice! Decide on a length that is not too tight and will allow the 2 ends to overlap at least 1″ and still feel comfortable. Write down that measurement.

2. Add ½″ to the measurement from Step 1.

3. Cut a strip of fabric and interfacing that is 2″ or 3″ or 4″ wide (refer to the note below) and the length from Step 2.

Note: Cut the fabric strip 4 times as wide as the measurement of the watch bar. For example, you need a width of 4″ for a 1″ watch bar, 3″ for a ¾″ watch bar, and 2″ for a ½″ watch bar.

You will love telling everyone what time it is with this super-adorable stitched watchband. Wrap it around your wrist a couple of times, or wrap it in some sweet paper as a gift for someone sweet!

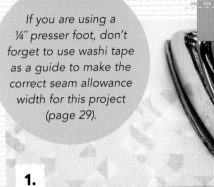

If you are using a ¼˝ presser foot, don't forget to use washi tape as a guide to make the correct seam allowance width for this project (page 29).

1.

Use an iron to fuse the interfacing to the back of the fabric strip.

2.

Fold in each end ½˝ and press with an iron.

3.

Fold the strip in half lengthwise, with wrong sides together. Press with an iron.

4.

Open out the strip so you can see the center crease and then fold in each long edge to meet the crease; then press with an iron.

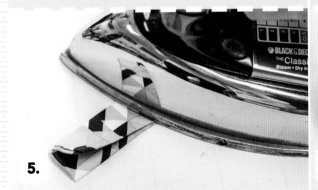

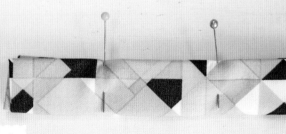

5.

Refold the strip on the crease, so the raw edges are on the inside, and press really well with an iron.

6.

Use some pins to hold the strip together while you are sewing.

Stitchy Stripy Watchband

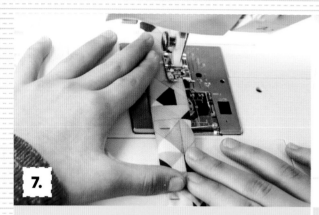

7.

Thread your sewing machine with fun-colored thread and stitch all the way around, nice and close to the edge.

8.

Use the sewing machine to sew your own crazy stripes up and down the strip. You could even experiment with some zigzag stripes.

Thread the strip through the bars on the watch face.

9.

Finish Up!

Using a snap-attaching tool and hammer, attach a snap to each end of the band. Make sure to read the instructions on the snap package!

Patchy Sewn Mirror

Finished Size: 9″ × 10″

What Do I Need?

- Various sizes of fabric scraps
- ⅓ yard of Peltex One-sided Fusible 71F interfacing (very stiff)
- 5″ × 5″ mirror plate or thrifted small mirror (You can find mirror plates in the candle section of arts and crafts stores.)
- 9″ × 10″ piece of felt
- Approximately 15″ of thick twine for hanging
- Bright fun-colored thread
- Hot glue gun
- Cardstock or cardboard
- Basic sewing supplies (page 10)

special skills

- Refer to The Rules of Sewing (page 7)
- Using a hot glue gun (page 21)
- Using an iron (page 19)
- Making and using templates (page 18)
- Sewing around a corner (page 17)

Prepare the pieces

1. Cut 2 pieces of fusible interfacing each to measure 9″ × 10″.

2. Cut a few strips of fabric in different widths between 1″ and 2½″ and several inches long. You won't need to worry about exact widths or lengths at this point. We will be following the idea of a Log Cabin quilting block for this. We will be working from a central piece and then adding strips to build outward.

TIP

It helps to lay all your strips out first, so you can get the placement sorted out. Remember that once you have sewn all the strips, it will end up a bit smaller.

3. Cut a central square or rectangle of fabric. You can cut it whatever size you want. I think a square around 2″ × 2″ or 3″ × 3″ works well.

4. Trace the mirror template pattern (page 132) onto heavy cardstock or cardboard and cut out the circle.

A super-cute mirror that is also totally portable. Make this for your friend who loves to travel! It measures approximately 9″ × 10″—the perfect size for your locker ... you will be too cool for school!

Let's Make It

If you are using a ¼″ presser foot, don't forget to use washi tape as a guide to make the correct seam allowance width for this project (page 29).

THE PATCHWORK FRONT

1. & 2.

Choose 1 of your cut strips. Place it on an edge of the center piece, with right sides together. Pin in place down the side.

Sew with the edge of the presser foot on the edge of the fabric.

3.

Open out the pieces and press flat with an iron. Trim off the excess fabric from the added strip to make an even edge.

4. & 5.

Add a piece to the other side of the center piece in the same way.

Open out the strip and press flat with an iron.

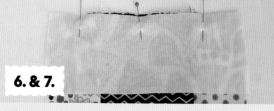

6. & 7.

Choose a strip as long as an edge of the piece you have sewn and as wide as you like.

Attach it by pinning it with right sides together along the top of the already-sewn strip.

8. & 9.

Sew along the long side with the edge of the presser foot on the edge of the fabric.

Open out the pieces and press flat with an iron.

10. Repeat Steps 6–9 to attach a strip to the bottom.

11. Continue adding strips around the edges until you have reached a size a little bigger than 9″ × 10″.

12. Press the entire piece with an iron. Make sure all the seams are flat on the back.

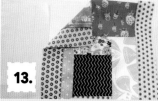

13.

Place the fusible interfacing on a flat surface, with the rough side facing up. Then center the patchy piece on top, with the wrong side down on the interfacing.

14. & 15.

Fuse the fabric to the interfacing with a hot iron.

Trim the excess fabric away from the interfacing edges.

WE LOVE TO SEW—GIFTS

16.

Use an erasable pen and the mirror circle template to draw a circle on the patchwork front. You can use the photo (page 53) as your guide, or you can decide where you think it looks best.

17.

Very carefully cut out the circle. Ask for help here if you need to.

TIP

Whenever I cut a circle from the middle of a piece of fabric or paper, I pinch a little fold of fabric right in the middle of the circle and snip it with a pair of scissors. This creates the perfect point for the tip of my scissors to start cutting.

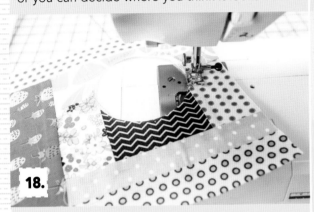

18.

Thread your machine with a bright, fun-colored thread and stitch around the edge of the cut circle. Use a straight stitch or a zigzag … it's your choice!

19. & 20.

Lay the patchwork front on a flat surface, with the fabric side facing down, and run a line of hot glue all around the edge of the cut-out circle. Make sure it is ½″–1″ from the edge (you don't want the glue to squeeze through and be visible!).

Press the mirror facedown onto the glue, making sure that it is centered over the cut circle. Wait a couple of minutes until the glue is dry.

THE BACK

Take your other piece of fusible interfacing and the felt for the backing and fuse them together in the same way that you fused the front (Steps 13–15, page 54).

Finish Up!

1. & 2.

Place the front and back pieces wrong sides together. Pin.

Insert the cut ends of the hanging twine between the front and back pieces on the top edge, ½″ from each side. Pin securely.

3.

Stitch all the way around with the edge of the presser foot on the edge of the fabric. It always helps to backstitch over the twine a couple of times just to make sure it is super secure.

Yo-Yo Garland

What Do I Need?

- Fabric scraps slightly larger than the pattern pieces (approximately 8″ × 8″ for the large yo-yo and 6″ × 6″ for the small yo-yo)

- Basic sewing supplies (page 10)

TIP

I have included patterns for 2 different sizes of yo-yo circles just in case you want to vary the design of the garland a little. The large finished yo-yo is approximately 3¼″ in diameter, and the small finished yo-yo is approximately 2¼″ in diameter.

special skills

- Refer to The Rules of Sewing (page 7)

- Making and using templates (page 18)

- Sewing a running stitch (page 23)

- Sewing a whipstitch (page 24)

Prepare the Pieces

Trace the large and small yo-yo template patterns (pullout page P1) on paper and cut out. Use the patterns to cut a few circles out of fabric in varying sizes.

Let's Make It

1. Thread an arm's length of button thread into the needle and knot the end about 2″ from the end.

Note: An arm's length of thread is measured from your fingertips to your shoulder. This makes the thread piece a little easier to manage.

2. Fold over the outer edges of the circle approximately ¼″ and use your finger to press a little crease. We will be folding the edge over as we go along. You may want to pin the fold down as you go; it is up to you.

Every day will be a celebration with this cute-as-a-button yo-yo garland. You will love making these fun yo-yo circles and sewing them into a fun strand to use for a party or give as the sweetest handmade gift ever!

3.

Find the center-ish of the folded seam allowance and bring the needle through the fabric from the front of the yo-yo to the back. We will be working with the yo-yo wrong side up.

4.

Start sewing a long ½˝ running stitch all the way around the circle, trying hard to keep your stitching in the center of the fold.

5.

When you get to the end, carefully pull both ends of the button thread to gather the circle in the middle, flattening and evening the gathering as you go along. Keep pulling and adjusting the gathers until you are happy with how it looks.

6. & 7.

Tie the thread tail to the other end of the thread, knot 4 times, and trim your threads. Smooth out the yo-yo with your hands just to get things nice and flat.

Make as many yo-yos as you need for your cute garland. Make it as short or as long as you want!

Finish Up!

1. & 2.

Arrange the yo-yos in the order you like.

Use an erasable pen to mark the joining spots on each yo-yo.

3.

Thread your needle with button thread and use a whipstitch to sew each yo-yo to its neighbor. Just a couple of stitches should do it, and be sure to knot everything off when you are done!

String up your garland and enjoy all that gorgeousness!

I Heart You Pillow

Finished Size: Approximately 12″ high

What Do I Need?

- ½ yard of fun decorator-weight fabric

- Fat quarter of fun fabric for the pocket (see Fat Quarter, page 28)

- Red perle cotton, size 8 *(optional)*

- Polyfill stuffing

- Basic sewing supplies (page 10)

If you are using a ¼″ presser foot, don't forget to use washi tape as a guide to make the correct seam allowance width for this project (page 29).

special skills

- Refer to The Rules of Sewing (page 7)

- Making and using templates (page 18)

- Sewing around a corner (page 17)

- Clipping curves (page 29)

- Sewing a backstitch (page 25)

- Sewing a whipstitch (page 24)

- Using an iron (page 19)

Prepare the Pieces

1. Trace the template patterns for the heart pillow and pillow pocket (pullout page P2).

2. Use the template to cut 2 heart pieces from the decorator-weight fabric.

3. Cut 1 piece of fabric for the back pocket.

Let's Make It

THE BACK POCKET

1. & 2.

Fold over the top edge of the back pocket ¼″ and iron.

Fold over another ¼″ and iron. Pin in place.

3. & 4.

Sew nice and close to the edge.

Trim any overhanging fabric from the side edges.

Optional: Use an erasable pen to write the word "love" (or any word) in cursive.

Backstitch with red perle cotton over all the letters.

Show your love with this soft and sweet heart pillow. Use the back pocket to store all those super-secret love letters.

1.

Lay the pocket right side up on top of a heart pillow piece, also right side up. Match the heart points and side edges. Pin the pocket in place.

2. & 3.

Place the front pillow piece (with the pocket pinned to it) and back pillow piece right sides together and pin all the way around.

Mark a 4″ no-sew zone on a straight side of the heart.

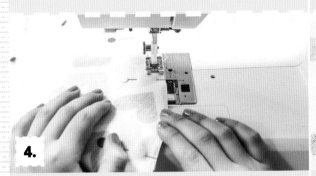

4.

Sew all the way around the heart with the edge of the presser foot on the edge of the fabric. Make sure to leave the no-sew zone open.

5.

Very carefully clip all the curved areas around the heart, particularly around the top and in the V of the heart.

6.

Turn the heart pillow right side out, push out all the seams, and press with an iron.

7. & 8.

Stuff the heart with plenty of polyfill stuffing.

Carefully whipstitch the opening closed.

I Heart You Pillow

Family Tree Wallhanging

Finished Size: Approximately 24½″ × 28″

What Do I Need?

- ¾ yard of 45″-wide cotton canvas fabric for the background
- ½ yard of quilt fabric for the tree foliage
- ¼ yard of quilt fabric for the tree trunk
- A scrap of bright-colored fabric for the bird's body
- Scraps of felt for the bird's eye and beak
- Felt to back the photos
- 1½ yards of paper-backed fusible web
- Fabric glue
- Home inkjet printer
- Inkjet printer fabric sheets (These can be found in packages online or at craft stores.)
- Wooden dowel for hanging
- Approximately 45″ of colored twine for hanging
- Sewing thread
- Basic sewing supplies (page 10)

special skills

- Refer to The Rules of Sewing (page 7)
- Using an iron (page 19)
- Hand sewing (page 23)
- Making and using templates (page 18)
- Using fusible web (page 20)

Prepare the Pieces

1. Trace the tree trunk, bird beak, bird eye, and bird body templates (pullout page P1). Tape the 2 pieces of the tree trunk and branches together to make a single piece. Transfer them and the 3 parts of the bird to the paper side of fusible web with a pencil. These templates are printed backward because they will be ironed to the wrong side of the fabric.

2. Following the manufacturer's instructions, iron the fusible web with the traced tree trunk to the wrong side of the tree trunk fabric. Cut around the trunk and set aside.

3. Following the manufacturer's instructions, iron the fusible web with the traced bird body to the wrong side of the bird fabric and cut it out. Iron the traced bird beak and eye to scraps of felt.

62

The perfect gift for that family you love. What could be better than a family tree to celebrate all that togetherness?

4. For the top of the tree, cut a 17″ × 17″ piece of paper-backed fusible web. Draw a rough circle to fill the entire piece of web. Don't worry if it's not perfect. I think a slightly wonky circle has more personality anyway!

5. Following the manufacturer's instructions, iron the fusible web to the back of the tree foliage fabric. Cut out the tree foliage circle.

6. Cut a 27″ × 30″ piece of cotton canvas.

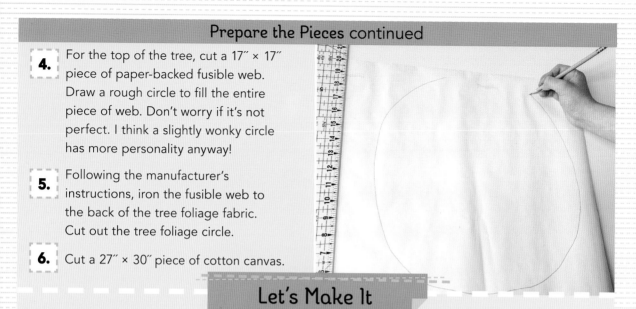

Let's Make It

THE CANVAS BACKGROUND

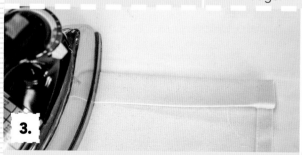

1. Fold in ½″ of the 27″-wide bottom edge of the cotton canvas and press with an iron.

2. Fold in another ½″ and pin in place. Sew nice and close to the folded edge. Repeat Steps 1 and 2 with both 30″ side edges of the canvas—pinning them in place and sewing nice and close to the edge.

3. Fold the top edge down ½″ and press with an iron. Now, fold the edge down 1″ and pin in place.

4. Stitch nice and close to the edge.

1.

Peel the backing paper off the tree trunk, the tree foliage, and the bird pieces.

2. & 3.

Position them on the canvas. Make sure they are positioned just the way you want them. Once they are ironed, they cannot be moved.

Fuse them in place with a hot iron.

4.

Stitch nice and close to the edge all the way around the tree sections. Sometimes it's easier to draw a sewing line with an erasable pen before you start sewing.

5.

Carefully stitch around the bird.

6.

Use a little fabric glue to attach the beak to the bird, because the beak is so small that it may be hard to stitch!

ADDING THE FAMILY TO THE TREE

1. Choose some digital photos of family members for the tree. These images will be printed onto an inkjet fabric sheet that measures 8½″ × 11″.

2. Pull up your chosen photos on the computer. Most computers allow you to edit your photos. Change the photo to black and white. It prints really well this

way. If you are not super tech savvy, ask for a little help from a grown-up.

3. Edit the image size so it is a size you like. I like my images to measure around 3″ tall.

4. Ask for help to put all your images on 1 page for printing (it saves inkjet sheets this way!). Once the photos look good, it's time to print your images.

Family Tree Wallhanging

5. Take all the other paper out of the printer and load an inkjet fabric sheet.

6. Print the images and then lay the sheet flat to dry for the time stated in the fabric sheet instructions, usually about 30 minutes.

7. Once the ink is dry, iron over the images to set the ink.

8. Cut around the photos. Cut pieces of felt the same sizes.

9.

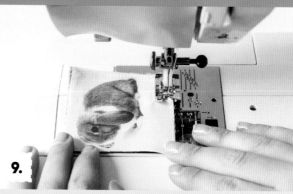

Place the felt pieces behind the photos and stitch all the way around close to the edge. I like to sew some decorative stitching around the images for a fun look.

10.

Hand stitch the photos to the tree. A simple little stitch will hold the pics in place and will be easy to unpick if you need to move things around later. (You may get a new brother, sister, or bunny!)

Finish Up!

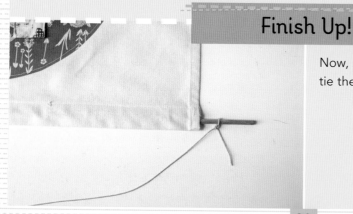

Now, slide the dowel into the upper casing and tie the colored twine on each end for hanging.

Oilcloth Tote with Fabric Handles

Finished Size: 7″ × 11″ × 4″

What Do I Need?

- ½ yard of oilcloth
- ½ yard of fabric for the lining
- ¼ yard of fabric for the handles
- ⅓ yard of interfacing
- 2½″ × 2½″ square of paper
- Large paper clips
- Basic sewing supplies (page 10)

special skills

- Refer to The Rules of Sewing (page 7)
- Using an iron (page 19)

Prepare the Pieces

1. Cut 2 pieces of oilcloth to measure 12½″ × 15″ each for the outside.

2. Cut 2 pieces of fabric to measure 12½″ × 15″ each for the lining.

3. Cut 2 pieces of fabric to measure 4″ × 15″ each for the handles.

4. Cut 2 pieces of interfacing to measure 4″ × 15″ each for the handles.

TIP

If your oilcloth fabric is a little wrinkly and crinkly, resist the urge to use an iron! Irons and oilcloth sure don't mix very well. Not only will your oilcloth be a melted mess, but your iron will be a mess too! Use a warm hairdryer held a few inches away to gently release the wrinkles. Be careful not to put it so close that the cloth starts to melt! After warming the oilcloth, I usually stack magazines on top until it has cooled.

Whether you use it as a lunch bag or a book bag, **this oilcloth tote will make you want to carry everything you can in it!** It is just so darn cute!

If you are using a ¼″ presser foot, don't forget to use washi tape as a guide to make the correct seam allowance width for this project (page 29).

THE OUTER BAG AND LINING

1.

Line up the 2½″ square piece of paper with the bottom corner of the oilcloth piece and trace around it with an erasable pen.

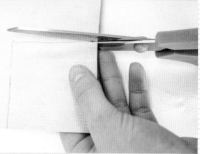

2. & 3.

Do the same with the other bottom corner of the oilcloth and the other oilcloth and fabric pieces.

Cut out on the marked lines.

4.

Place the oilcloth pieces right sides together and secure with paper clips along the sides and across the bottom.

TIP

Do not use pins to hold oilcloth together. Pins will leave permanent holes. Use paper clips instead.

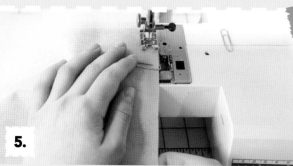

5.

Sew down the sides and along the bottom with the edge of the presser foot on the edge of the fabric. Make sure not to sew in the cut-out corners.

TIP

To make sewing on oilcloth a little easier, take the presser foot off your machine and place some masking or washi tape on the bottom of the foot. Be sure to trim off all the excess tape and use a pin to tear away the tape that is in the hole where the needle needs to go.

Now you have an inner and an outer bag all sewn and ready to go!

6.

Bring the side and bottom seams together at both bottom cut-out corners of the bag. Place the seams so they will lie right on top of each other. The cut-out square will become a straight line with the side and bottom seams in the middle. Paper clip the raw edges together.

7. – 9.

Repeat Step 6 with the other side as well and paper clip in place.

Sew both corners with the edge of the presser foot on the edge of the fabric.

Repeat these steps with the lining pieces.

THE HANDLES

1.

Lay the fusible interfacing on the wrong side of each of the handle pieces. Then trim all the way around to make sure there is no overhanging interfacing. Iron to fuse the interfacing in place.

2.

Fold the handle piece in half lengthwise with wrong sides together and press with an iron.

3.

Open it out so you can see the center crease; then fold a side in to meet the crease and press.

4.

Fold in the other side to the center crease and press.

Oilcloth Tote with Fabric Handles

THE HANDLES continued

5.

Refold the strip on the crease so the raw edges are on the inside and press in place.

6.

It is a good idea to use some pins to hold everything in place.

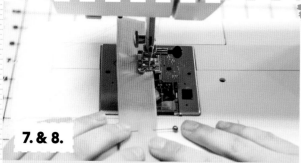

7. & 8.

Sew nice and close to the edge down both sides of the handle.

Repeat this for the other handle.

TIP

It is sometimes easier to draw a sewing line with an erasable pen when you are sewing a line that is not sewn with the edge of the presser foot on the edge of the fabric.

PUT IT ALL TOGETHER

1.

Keep the lining piece inside out, fold over the top to the outside 1″, and press.

2.

Turn the oilcloth outer bag right side out and fold over the top to the inside 1″ and finger-press. Do not put the iron anywhere near the oilcloth or it will become a melted mess!

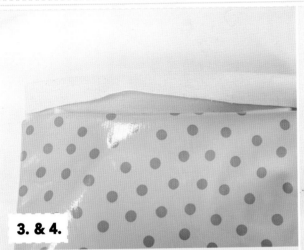

3. & 4.

Place the lining bag (inside out) in the oilcloth bag (right side out) and line up the side seams.

Using paper clips, clip the lining and outer bag together.

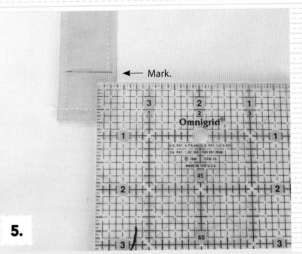

← Mark.

5.

Mark 1″ from the ends of each of the handles.

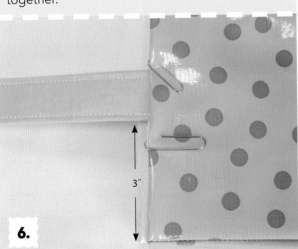

3″

6.

Measure in 3″ from the side seam of the bag and mark. Insert an end of the handle between the lining and the oilcloth at the 3″ mark and push the end in only as far as that 1″ mark. Use a paper clip to hold the handle securely in place. Repeat for the other end of the handle, placing it 3″ in from the other side seam. Do this with both handles.

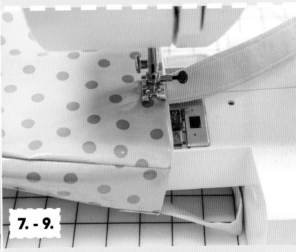

7. - 9.

Carefully and slowly sew around the top of the bag, removing the clips as you get to them.

Sew carefully over the handle area; you don't want to get the handles all caught up.

Trim your threads and shout "Hooray!" You are all done!

Super-Sweet-Smelling Lavender Sachets

Finished Size: Approximately 4¾″ × 6½″

What Do I Need?

- Large scrap at least 6″ × 15″ or ¼ yard of cotton fabric for the outer bag (You can make 3 bags with ¼ yard.)

- Large scrap at least 5″ × 14″ of muslin for the inner bag

- ⅛ yard of fun-colored cotton for the ties

- Dried lavender (about 1 cup)

- Basic sewing supplies (page 10)

special skills

- Refer to The Rules of Sewing (page 7)

- Using an iron (page 19)

Prepare the Pieces

1. Cut 1 piece of cotton fabric to measure 5½″ × 14″ for the outer bag.

2. Cut 1 piece of muslin to measure 4½″ × 13″ for the inner bag.

3. Cut 2 pieces of cotton to measure 2″ × 22½″ for the ties.

If you are using a ¼″ presser foot, don't forget to use washi tape as a guide to make the correct seam allowance width for this project (page 29).

Let's Make It

THE INNER BAG

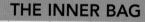

1.

Fold both short ends of the piece of muslin in ½″ and press with an iron.

There is something about the smell of lavender that makes me feel happy. Now it's time to spread the happiness and **make these sweet-smelling lavender sachets for all your friends.** Pop one in your pillow for sweet dreams or stash it in your drawer to keep your clothes smelling fresh ... Mmmmmm.

75

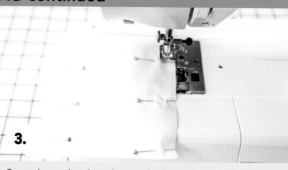

2.

Fold the piece of fabric in half crosswise and pin down both sides, making sure to keep the folded ends on the outside.

3.

Sew down both sides with the edge of the presser foot on the edge of the fabric.

4.

Turn the muslin lining right side out and fill with lavender. Make sure you do not overfill the bag.

5. & 6.

Pin the opening closed.

Sew along the edge of the bag nice and close to the edge.

THE OUTER BAG

1.

Fold in both short ends of the main fabric piece ¼″, then fold ¼″ again, and press with an iron.

2.

Stitch down the fold nice and close to the edge.

3.

With the right side of the fabric facing up, use an erasable pen to mark 1¼″ in from each long side of the fabric piece.

1.

Fold the piece of tie fabric in half lengthwise, wrong sides together, and press with an iron.

2.

Open out the fabric strip and fold in each end ¼″ and press. Next fold in a side to meet the center crease and press with an iron.

3.

Fold in the other side to meet the center crease and press with an iron.

4.

Refold the strip on the crease so the raw edges are on the inside and press with an iron.

5.

Sew the ties around all 4 sides nice and close to the edge.

6.

Place a tie along the inner side of the marks on the fabric piece. Make sure that roughly the same length of the tie extends beyond the fabric at both ends. Repeat with the other tie, placing it along the other mark.

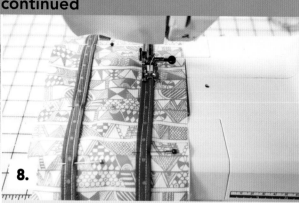

7.

Pin the ties in place.

8.

Sew on top of the previous stitch lines down both sides, backstitching at the beginning and end.

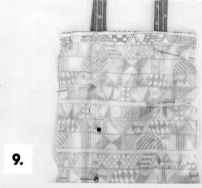

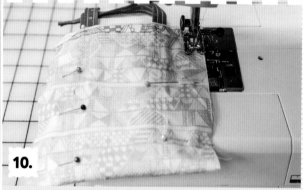

9.

Fold the outer bag piece in half with right sides together and pin down both sides.

10.

Sew down both sides with the edge of the foot on the edge of the fabric.

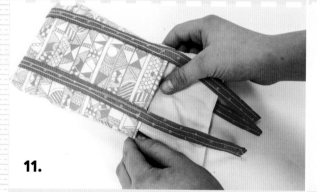

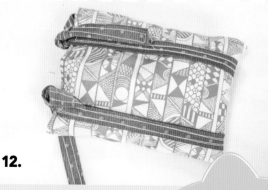

11.

Turn the bag right side out.

12.

Place the lavender sachet inside the bag and tie the ties neatly.

Make a whole stack for all your friends!

Super-Cute Gadget Case

Finished Size: Approximately 9¼″ × 12¼″

What Do I Need?

- Fat quarter of quilting fabric for the outer case (see Fat Quarter, page 28)

- Fat quarter of cotton fabric for the lining

- ⅛ yard of fabric for the handle

- 15″ × 24″ of cotton quilt batting

- 10″ of colored ribbon or elastic (½″–1″ wide)

- 2 metal clasps called trigger snap hooks (These can be found in a hardware store.)

- Button, ⅝″–¾″ size (You may want to wait to choose the button until after sewing the bag to be sure you have a button that will fit in the loop.)

- Basic sewing supplies (page 10)

TIP

Look for a quilting fabric with a geometric design or even a fun plaid or check. You will be stitching on the fabric, and it looks super cute if you have a bold pattern to follow.

special skills

- Refer to The Rules of Sewing (page 7)
- Using an iron (page 19)
- Sewing on a button (page 22)
- Sewing around a corner (page 17)

Prepare the Pieces

1. Cut 2 pieces of outer fabric to measure 10″ × 13″ each.

2. Cut 2 pieces of batting to measure 12″ × 15″ each.

3. Cut 2 pieces of lining fabric to measure 10″ × 13″ each.

4. Cut 1 piece of handle fabric to measure 2″ × 40″.

5. Cut 3 pieces of colored ribbon or elastic to measure 3″ each for the handles and closure.

TIP

Cut the outer fabric and lining fabric as shown. It will not fit if the pieces face in the other direction.

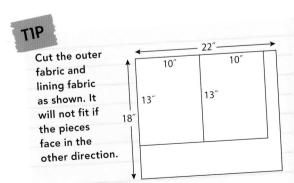

79

Whether it's for a tablet or an e-reader or even just used as a sweet little purse, **everyone will love this cute and handy bag!**

Let's Make It

If you are using a ¼″ presser foot, don't forget to use washi tape as a guide to make the correct seam allowance width for this project (page 29).

THE CASE

1.

Lay the outer fabric on top of the batting piece and pin in place.

2.

Machine stitch over lines in the print of the fabric or use an erasable marker to draw your own simple geometric design or simple lines. It's up to you!

3. & 4.

Once you have finished, trim off the extra batting so that the fabric and batting are the same size.

Repeat Steps 1–3 with the other piece of fabric and batting.

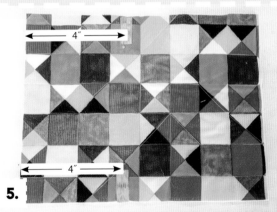

4″

4″

5.

Fold 2 of the 3″ ribbon or elastic pieces in half crosswise. Measure 4″ up from the bottom of both sides of the outer bag fabric and pin a folded ribbon so that the raw edges are lined up and the fold faces toward the middle of the bag. It may seem strange to put it in this way, but I promise it will all make sense in the end. Be sure to put the pins perpendicular to the edge so you can easily remove them later. Repeat on the other side of the bag.

Super Cute Gadget Case

6.

Place the outer fabric pieces right sides together.

7.

Pin them together around 3 sides; leave a short end open.

8. & 9.

Sew around the 3 sides with the edge of the presser foot on the edge of the fabric. The ribbon will be sewn in this seam.

Turn the outer bag right side out and press with an iron.

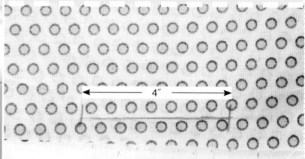

4″

10. & 11.

Pin the lining pieces right sides together, leaving the top open.

Mark a 4″ no-sew zone in the bottom for turning.

Sew around the 3 sides, but don't forget the no-sew zone!

Measure exactly halfway across the top opening of the outer bag and mark the halfway point.

Pin a folded piece of ribbon or elastic to the marked spot. Make sure the loop is facing down with the raw edges lined up.

12. - 14.

82

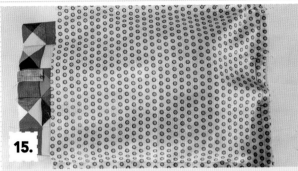

15. With the outer bag right side out and the lining inside out, slide the outer bag inside the lining.

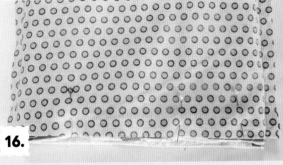

16. Pin around the top of the bag. I find it easier to pin at the side seams first.

17. If you have an open-arm sewing machine, pull the extension table off your machine and slide the top of the bag on the machine. You will be sewing around in a circle. Start sewing around the top with the edge of the presser foot on the edge of the fabric. Stop when you get around to where you started.

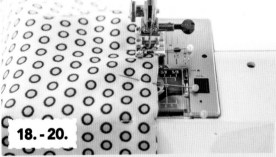

18. - 20. Pull the bag right side out through the hole at the bottom of the lining.

Pin the hole closed and sew close to the edge.

Push the lining inside the bag, making sure to push out all the corners.

THE HANDLE

1. Fold the handle fabric strip in half lengthwise with wrong sides together. Press with an iron.

2. Open out the strip so you can see the crease and fold in each long edge to meet the center crease. Press with an iron.

3.

Refold the strip on the center crease so the raw edges are on the inside and press really well with an iron.

4.

Use pins to hold the strip together while you are sewing.

5.

Sew down both sides nice and close to the edge of the fabric.

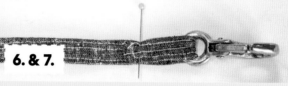

6. & 7.

Loop an end of the handle through the loop on the clasp and pull it through about 1″. Sew the handle in place, being sure to backstitch a few times to make it extra secure. Repeat with the other end of the handle.

Clip the clasps to the elastic or ribbon loops.

Finish Up!

Fold the bag top over and mark the spot for the button. Choose a button that will comfortably fit through the elastic or ribbon loop and sew the button in place. How do I sew a button? Go to Sewing on a Button (page 22) to find out!

Cozy Pet Bed

Finished Size: approximately 26″ × 26″

What Do I Need?

- 1⅝ yards of heavy decorator-weight fabric
- 26″ × 26″ pillow form
- 1 ball of yarn for pom-poms
- Pinking shears (*optional—refer to the tip, page 88*)
- Basic sewing supplies (page 10)

special skills

- Refer to The Rules of Sewing (page 7)
- Using an iron (page 19)
- Making pom-poms (page 21)
- Sewing around a corner (page 17)

Prepare the Pieces

1. Cut 1 piece of fabric to measure 26¾″ × 26¾″ for the front.

2. Cut 2 pieces of fabric to measure 19″ × 26¾″ for the back.

TIP

Cut the pieces as shown. This is especially important if your fabric is narrower than 54″.

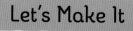

If you are using a ¼″ presser foot, don't forget to use washi tape as a guide to make the correct seam allowance width for this project (page 29).

Let's Make It

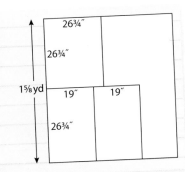

1.

Fold in a long end of each back piece ½″. Then fold in another ½″ and press with an iron.

All pets need a cozy place to sleep. Here is your chance to make your kitty, your pooch, or even your bunny a bed worthy of wagging-tail royalty!

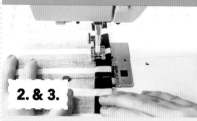

2. & 3.

Pin the folds in place.

Sew nice and close to the folded edge on both back pieces.

4. & 5.

Lay the front pillow piece right side up on a flat surface.

Lay a pillow back piece right side facing down on the main piece. Line up the raw edges on 3 sides and pin in place.

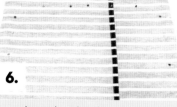

6.

Lay the other back piece on top. Line up the raw edges on 3 sides. The folded edge will overlap the folded edge of the other backing piece, but that's okay. Pin around all 4 sides of the pillow.

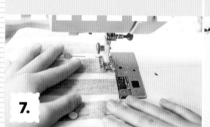

7.

Sew around all 4 sides of the pillow with the edge of the presser foot on the edge of the fabric.

8.

Use pinking shears to cut around all the raw fabric edges. This will stop them from fraying. Just don't cut the stitches!

TIP

If you don't have pinking shears, you can set your sewing machine to a zigzag stitch and zigzag close to the edge around the entire pillow.

9. Trim the corners, being careful not to cut into the stitching.

10. Turn your pet pillow right side out and give it a good press with an iron.

Finish Up!

1. & 2.

Make 4 pom-poms.

Thread a needle with button thread and push it through the corner of the pillow. Tie a knot.

We sewed some fun pom-poms to the corners of our pet beds just to add that something special!

3.

Push the needle through the center of the pom-pom and then back through the corner of the pillow. Repeat this a couple more times until the pom-pom is secure.

4. - 6.

Tie a double knot with the thread ends.

Repeat Steps 2–4 with the other 3 corners.

Put the pillow form inside the cover and prepare for your pet to sleep tight!

Squeaky Dog Bone

What Do I Need?

- ¼ yard of canvas-type fabric
- Dog toy squeaker (available at pet stores and online)
- Polyester stuffing
- Basic sewing supplies (page 10)

special skills

- Refer to The Rules of Sewing (page 7)
- Using an iron (page 19)
- Making and using templates (page 18)
- Sewing a whipstitch (page 24)
- Sewing around a corner (page 17)

Prepare the Pieces

1. Use the Dog Bone pattern (page 131) to cut 1 complete bone piece from the canvas fabric. The pattern shows only half a bone. To make a full bone template, fold a large piece of paper in half, place the fold on the dotted center line of the pattern, and trace. Cut out the template and open it up.

2. Cut another piece of canvas to measure 8″ × 15″ for the backing.

Let's Make It

1.

Lay the fabric bone on top of the backing fabric with right sides together and pin in place.

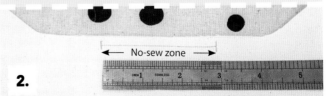

← No-sew zone →

2.

Mark a 3″ no-sew zone along a straight edge of the bone (refer to the pattern piece for the markings).

89

This is a great project to make for your four-legged friend, or you could even grab a group of friends and make a stack for your local SPCA or animal shelter!

I'm sure your pup loves to play and chew his toys all day long. **Think how much she will love to chew on a toy made by you!**

3.

Sew all the way around with the edge of the presser foot on the edge of the fabric. Make sure not to sew in the no-sew zone! There are lots of curves here, so be sure to sew slowly and pivot carefully when you are sewing around the sharp corners in both ends.

4.

Carefully cut around the bone to remove the excess backing fabric.

5.

Use the tips of the scissors to snip every 1″ around the curved section of the bone. This will help the bone keep its curved shape when you pull it right side out. Be very careful not to clip into the stitching!

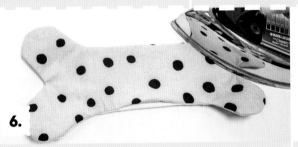

6.

Pull the bone right side out, making sure to push out all the little nooks and crannies.

7.

Tightly stuff each end of the bone with stuffing.

8.

When you have added ¾ of the stuffing, stop and pop the squeaker through the hole. Continue stuffing, making sure there is stuffing all around the squeaker.

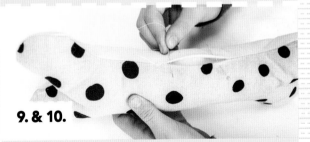

9. & 10.

Pin the opening closed.

Carefully whipstitch the opening closed with button thread and securely knot the thread at the end.

Embroidered Pet Portraits

What Do I Need?

- Inkjet printer fabric sheets (most measure 8½″ × 11″ and can be found in packages online or at a fabric store)

- Inkjet printer

- 8″ wood embroidery hoop

- Embroidery floss or perle cotton (size 8)

- Small beads *(optional)* (Make sure your needle can pass through the hole in the beads. If it is too tight, you may need a larger bead!)

- Basic sewing supplies (page 10)

special skills

- Refer to The Rules of Sewing (page 7)
- Using an iron (page 19)
- Hand sewing (page 23)

Let's Make It

THE IMAGE

1. Choose a digital photo of your favorite pet. You will be printing the image onto fabric, so it is important to make sure that everything is prepared correctly before you start the printing. Ask an adult if you need help.

2. Pull up the photo on the computer. Change the photo to black and white using the editing feature. It prints really well this way. Resize the photo so that the image of your pet will fit into an 8″ embroidery hoop.

3. Remove all the regular paper from your inkjet printer and load the inkjet fabric sheet into the paper tray. Following the manufacturer's instructions, print your photo onto the fabric.

Immortalize your favorite pooch, bunny, kitty, or even lizard with these beyond-cute pet portraits. Make one for the pet lover in your life (and one for yourself!).

THE IMAGE continued

4. Lay your printed image flat to dry for the time stated in the fabric sheet instructions, usually about 30 minutes.

5. Once the image is dry, use an iron with the steam turned off to iron over the image to set the ink.

THE EMBROIDERY

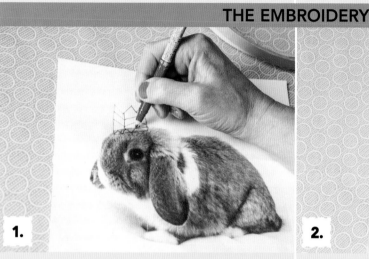

1.

2.

Use an erasable pen to mark your embroidery design on the fabric. Try not to press too hard, because you do not want to damage the print. Be creative but don't make the design too complicated. Make each part of your design simple; you can add beads later!

Peel the paper from the back of the photo fabric.

Hoop the fabric. Don't worry if it's not perfectly centered—you can go back and rehoop it later.

How to Use an Embroidery Hoop

1. Loosen the little screw on top of the wood embroidery hoop. Separate the 2 hoops.

2. Place the inner hoop on a flat surface and lay the printed fabric on top with the image in the position you like.

3. Lay the loosened outer ring on top of the inner ring and push it down so that it firmly attaches on the outside.

4. Tighten the screw so that the fabric is held firmly in place.

Stitch on the Pet Photo

Use the stitch of your choice to embroider the design.

- Running stitch (page 23)
- Backstitch (page 25)
- Vicki knot (page 26)

For this project, we will be using a large backstitch.

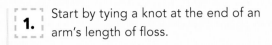

1. Start by tying a knot at the end of an arm's length of floss.

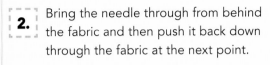

2. Bring the needle through from behind the fabric and then push it back down through the fabric at the next point.

3.

Bring the needle up again at the next point.

4.

Now go backward and push it back down at the last point to fill in the line.

5.

Continue stitching this way until the entire crown is filled.

6.

Carefully iron the crown to remove the erasable pen.

This is your project. Experiment with embroidery— I'm sure it will look great!

ADDING BEADS

1. Thread your needle with embroidery floss or perle cotton.

2. Tie a knot in the end.

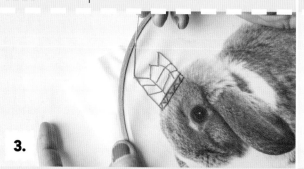

3.

Bring the needle through the fabric from behind.

4.

Thread a small bead in the needle.

5.

Take the needle back down to the back of the fabric and bring the needle back up at the next position.

6. & 7.

Continue doing this until you have finished your design.

Tie a knot close to the back of the fabric when you get to the end.

Finish Up!

If you want to center the photo better, loosen the hoop screw, adjust the fabric, and retighten the screw. Trim around the fabric on the back of the hoop.

Hang your glorious portrait!

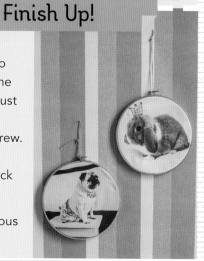

Super Dog Collar

What Do I Need?

- ¾ yard of nylon webbing (1″ wide)
- ⅛ yard of fabric
- Fun-colored sewing thread
- Adjustable plastic side-release or parachute buckle (1″) (You can buy these at a craft store, or you can reuse these parts from an old collar!)
- Plastic slider buckle (1″)
- 2 metal D-rings (1″)
- Basic sewing supplies (page 10)

special skills

- Refer to The Rules of Sewing (page 7)
- Using an iron (page 19)

Prepare the Pieces

1. Cut the fabric to measure 3½″ × 28½″.

2. Ask an adult to gently burn both ends of the webbing using a butane lighter. This will prevent fraying.

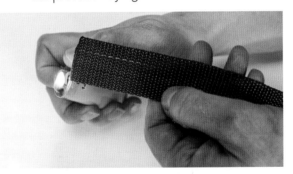

Let's Make It

1.

Fold in each end of the fabric strip ½″ and press with an iron.

97

No shopping at the pet store for you. **You are going to learn to make your very own, totally custom pet collar!**

2.

Fold the strip in half lengthwise with wrong sides together and press with an iron.

3.

Open out the strip so you can see the crease and fold in each long edge to meet the center crease. Press with an iron.

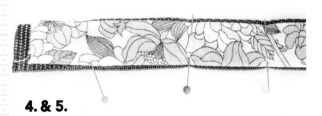

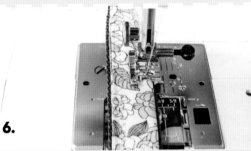

4. & 5.

Refold the strip on the crease so the raw edges are on the inside and press really well with an iron.

Center the fabric piece on the nylon webbing and pin.

6.

Stitch around the entire piece. Why not use a fun zigzag stitch?

7.

Take an end of the webbing and attach half of the side-release buckle by threading the webbing above the plastic bar and then going back down through to the back. Make sure the buckle is facing up.

8. & 9.

Pull the webbing out a couple of inches.

Use an erasable pen to mark a line 1″ from the buckle. Sew on that line through both layers of webbing to attach the buckle.

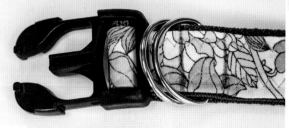

10.

Slide the D-rings onto the webbing up to the stitched line. Mark another line ½″ from the D-rings and stitch on the line through both layers of webbing. This will hold the D-rings in place.

11.

Slide the slider buckle on the other end of the webbing and move it down a few inches.

12.

Now thread the other half of the side-release buckle onto the webbing in the same way as you did for the first half in Step 7.

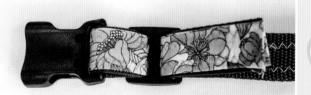

13.

Pull a few inches of webbing through both the side-release buckle and the slider buckle. This helps make the collar adjustable.

Now all you have to do is choose which pet gets to wear this super-sweet collar. Here's a thought: why not make matching collars for all your four-legged friends?

Kitty Catnip Toy

What Do I Need?

- 6″ × 8″ piece of felt for each fish body
- 5″ × 5″ piece of felt for the scales of 1 fish
- Colored embroidery floss for the eyes
- ¼″ or ½″ dowel (can be purchased at a craft or hardware store)
- Dried catnip (can be purchased at a pet supply store)
- Polyester stuffing
- Approximately 24″ of twine
- Fun-colored sewing machine thread
- Basic sewing supplies (page 10)

special skills

- Refer to The Rules of Sewing (page 7)
- Using an iron (page 19)
- Making and using templates (page 18)
- Sewing a Vicki knot (page 26)

Prepare the Pieces

1. Use the patterns to make templates (Kitty Toy patterns, page 130).

2. Cut 2 fish bodies for each fish.

3. Cut 8 sets of scales for each fish.

Let's Make It

1.

Measure 2″ from the top point of the fish body and draw a line.

2. Draw 3 more lines, each ½″ under the previous line. You should now have 4 lines. These are the fish-scale placement lines.

You cannot go wrong with this fishy-shaped kitty toy! Add some catnip and it will be your kitty's favorite plaything!

3.

Place a row of fish scales under the bottom line and stitch in place across the top of the scales.

4.

Attach another row of scales under the next line.

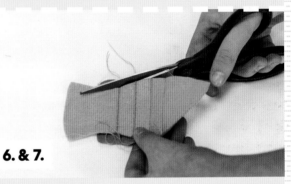

5.

Continue until you have 4 rows of scales sewn onto the fish body. I used a fun zigzag stitch for the top set of scales.

6. & 7.

Trim any overhanging scales, using the edges of the fish body as your guide.

Repeat Steps 1–6 to add the other scales to the other fish body piece.

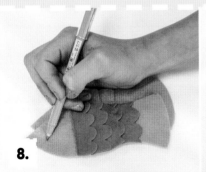

8.

Decide where you want to place the eyes and mark with an erasable pen.

9.

Sew a Vicki knot (page 26) to each fish body piece for the eye.

10.

Place the fish body pieces wrong sides together and pin in place.

11.

Sew around the fish close to the edge. Be sure to leave a no-sew zone about 1˝ long at the bottom of the fish.

TIP

Try to sew from the top to the bottom in the direction of the fish scales. It will be way easier, and you will be less likely to get the scales all bunched up under the presser foot.

12.

Stuff the fish with a little stuffing; then add a spoonful of dried catnip.

Add some more stuffing until the fish is filled.

13.

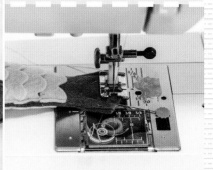

Pin the bottom of the fish closed and sew near the edge to close up the opening.

Finish Up!

Make as many fish as you like. Thread some embroidery floss through the top of each fish and tie them securely on the end of a wooden dowel.

Tie on some yarn or maybe a feather or two, and your cat will be the luckiest kitty on the block!

Gifts for Your School Friends

Felt Heart Paper-Clip Set

What Do I Need?

- Scraps of felt
- Fun-colored perle cotton #8 or embroidery floss separated into 3 strands
- Paper clip
- Polyester stuffing
- Basic sewing supplies (page 10)

special skills

- Refer to The Rules of Sewing (page 7)
- Using an iron (page 19)
- Making and using templates (page 18)
- Sewing a running stitch (page 23)

Prepare the Pieces

1. Make templates using the patterns (Felt Paper Clip patterns, page 133).

2. Trace the template pieces onto the felt with an erasable pen. You will need 2 of each shape.

Let's Make It

1. Mark dots with an erasable pen every ¼″ around 1 piece of each shape. This will help your running stitch stay even.

2. Pin the pairs of pieces together.

These heart paper clips show the love and are practical too! Use them to control your clutter or mark your spot in your favorite book. In fact, why not make a few for your favorite teacher?

107

3. & 4.

Tie a knot in the perle cotton or floss, about 2″ from the end.

Bring the needle through from the back of the felt. Sew a running stitch all the way around the shape but leave a small 1″-long opening to stuff it. Do not knot the thread yet. Let the thread and needle hang loose for now.

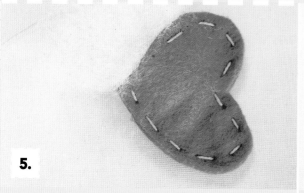

5.

Use tiny tufts of stuffing to fatten the little shape.

6.

Continue stitching to close the opening. Tie a double knot at the end with both ends of the perle cotton or floss.

Finish Up!

Attach the shape to the paper clip with a little stitch that will run through the top of the paper clip and the middle back of the shape.

Use these paper clips as bookmarks or to hold that stack of pesky papers together!

Covered-Button Pushpins

What Do I Need?

- Small fabric scraps
- Flat-back pushpins (thumbtacks)
- Hot glue gun (low temperature)
- Covered-button set (½˝)
- Pliers

special skills

- Using a hot glue gun (page 21)

Let's Make It

Most covered-button sets come with instructions and the tools to make a covered button. Read the instructions on the package before starting.

1. Ask for help from an adult to remove the wire loop found on the bottom of the covered button pieces. Pliers should do the job pretty quickly.

2. Cut a piece of fabric that is bigger than the button you want to cover.

109

Gather all your inspiration on one board with these adorable pushpins. Make them to perfectly match your or your bestie's personal space. Pinning has never been so fun!

3. & 4.

Lay the fabric with the print side down on top of the rubber button-making base.

Press the upper button piece into the rubber piece, with the curved top facing down.

5. & 6.

Trim any fabric that overhangs the rubber base.

Fold the remaining edges into the button top.

7.

Place the other button piece on top of the folded-in fabric and use the round plastic button-making tool to press the button base down hard to click into the outer button.

8.

Pull the finished button out of the rubber base and you have 1 all done!

When you have made all your buttons, it's time to attach the pushpins.

9.

Carefully add a dab of hot glue to the top of each flat-back pushpin (thumbtack) and attach it securely to the button underside.

10.

Wait for the glue to dry.

Make a whole ton of pins and give them as a gift, pushed into a piece of cork.

Covered Button Pushpins

Scrappy Patchy Pencil Cup

What Do I Need?

- Scraps at least 7″ long of fun fabric

- Mason jar (We used a jar measuring 6½″ tall, but you can use any size for this project.)

- ¼ yard of plain canvas fabric for the backing

- Fun-colored sewing machine thread

- Basic sewing supplies (page 10)

special skills

- Refer to The Rules of Sewing (page 7)
- Using an iron (page 19)

Prepare the Pieces

1. Use a tape measure to measure the jar from the base to just under the lid area. Now add ½″ and write that measurement down. It will be the height of your cover. (My jar measures 5½″, with the addition of ½″ to make a measurement of 6″.)

2. Measure around the circumference of the jar. Add ¾″ and write down the measurement. (Mine is 12¼″, with the addition of ¾″ to make a measurement of 13″.)

3. Cut the canvas the height and width of the measurements that you wrote down in Steps 1 and 2. (In my case, 6″ × 13″.)

4. Cut a variety of fabric scraps a bit longer than the height (in my case, approximately 6½″) and to whatever width you like.

Everyone needs somewhere
to put stray pens and pencils.
**What's better than this
super-cool patchy pencil cup?**
Maybe they will make you want
to spend more time writing ...

If you are using a ¼" presser foot, don't forget to use washi tape as a guide to make the correct seam allowance width for this project (page 29).

1.

Start by placing the first fabric right side up along an end of the canvas and pin. Stitch it down close to the long fabric edge at the end of the canvas.

2.

Lay the second strip right side down on top of the first strip, so that the long edges are lined up; pin.

3.

Sew with the edge of the presser foot on the long edge of the fabric strip.

4. & 5.

Open out the strip and press with an iron.

Lay the third strip right side down on the second strip and sew in the same way. Open out to press. Continue until the entire canvas piece is covered with fabric strips.

6.

Iron the entire piece well.

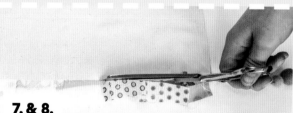

7. & 8.

Secure the last strip by sewing down close to the outer edge.

Turn the piece over and trim it even with the canvas edges.

9.

Time to do some fun stitching! Take this moment to explore some other stitches on your machine and get creative stitching over seams.

Finish Up!

1.

Fold the top under ¼" and press with an iron.

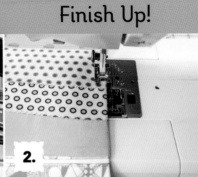

2.

Sew close to the edge.

3.

Fold the bottom under ¼". Press with an iron and sew close to the edge.

4.

Fold the finished piece in half, right sides facing, and pin the ends together.

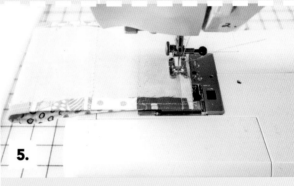

5.

Sew with the edge of the foot on the edge of the fabric.

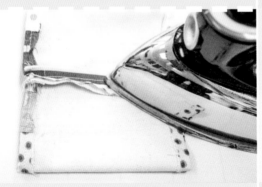

6.

Press the seam open with an iron.

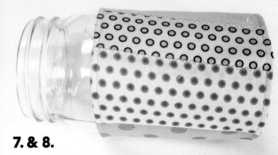

7. & 8.

Trim off all those pesky threads and turn it right side out.

Slide the sleeve onto the mason jar.

What a great transformation!

Stitchy Coil Trinket Bowl

What Do I Need?

- Cotton clothesline (can be found in a hardware store)
- Gluestick
- ¼ yard of quilting-weight fabric
- Fun-colored thread
- Basic sewing supplies (page 10)

special skills

- Refer to The Rules of Sewing (page 7)

Prepare the Pieces

Cut strips of fabric ½″ × the full width of the fabric, selvage to selvage. You should only need around 4 or 5 strips.

Let's Make It

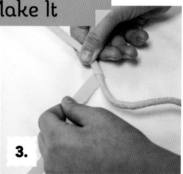

1. & 2.

Cut a piece of clothesline approximately 75″ long.

Apply some glue to the tip of a fabric strip.

3.

Glue the strip to the cotton clothesline and begin wrapping the fabric around the clothesline on an angle, making sure to wrap tightly and with the fabric strip overlapping each time around the clothesline.

4. When you get to the end of a fabric strip, simply apply some glue and then start on a new strip.

5. Continue wrapping until you have filled the length of clothesline.

This bowl is perfect for storing all your favorite little **trinkets.** Give it as a gift with a sweet little treat inside!

6.

Coil an end of the cord around until you have a circle that is about 8 coils across. Push pins through at 4 points around the circle to hold the coils in place.

7.

Sew all the way across the coil base in a straight line, starting and ending with a backstitch.

8. & 9.

Sew straight across again, to form a cross. Don't forget to backstitch!

Now sew straight across again between the other lines. It looks a bit like a star now!

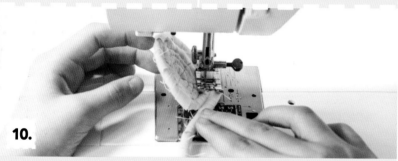

10.

Now it is time to start sewing the sides of the bowl. Adjust your machine so you are sewing a wide zigzag stitch.

Tilt the coil base slightly on its side and, while holding it on its side, start zigzag stitching the cord around the sides of the bowl. You want each zigzag stitch to catch both sides of the coil so they become sewn together.

11.

Try hard to keep the rows of cording touching as you sew around.

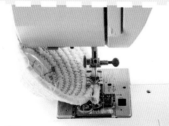

12.

Continue while holding the bowl at an angle as shown in the photo until you have finished. Make sure to backstitch at the end so that the end is super secure.

How cute is this crafty bowl? There are so many possibilities with this fun technique! Work with a longer piece of clothesline and make a larger bowl, or maybe make a teeny tiny one to hold some tiny treasures!

Let's Wrap It Up

119

Sewn Gift Bags

Finished Size: Approximately 7¾″ × 9⅝″

What Do I Need?

- Fat quarter of fun fabric (see Fat Quarter, page 28)

- Approximately 24″ of fun-colored twine

- Basic sewing supplies (page 10)

special skills

- Refer to The Rules of Sewing (page 7)

- Using an iron (page 19)

- Sewing around a corner (page 17)

Prepare the Pieces

Cut 2 pieces of fabric 8½″ × 12″ using the diagram as your guide.

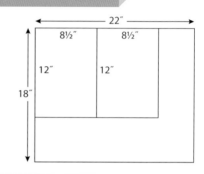

If you are using a ¼″ presser foot, don't forget to use washi tape as a guide to make the correct seam allowance width for this project (page 29).

Let's Make It

1.

Place the 2 fabric pieces right sides together and pin down a long (12″) side.

2.

Sew down that side with the edge of the presser foot on the edge of the fabric.

With these fun fabric gift bags, **wrapping your gift can be almost as much fun as making it.** They have a great dual purpose of holding your gift and then being a useful little bag for storing special things!

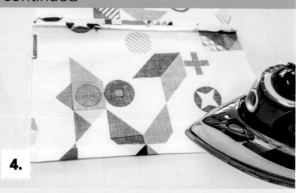

3.

Open out the seam and iron it flat.

4.

Fold in ½″ on each of the remaining 12″-long sides and press with an iron.

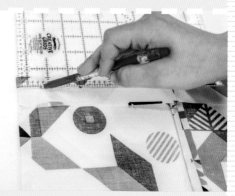

5.

Fold down the top 1½″ and press with an iron.

6.

Use an erasable-ink pen to draw a line ½″ from the top folded edge. Extend the line to go from side to side across the entire top.

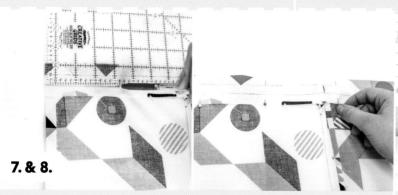

7. & 8.

Draw another line ½″ under the first line.

Pin the top folded edge down to hold it in place while you sew.

9.

Sew on both lines, making sure to backstitch at the beginning and end.

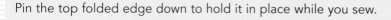

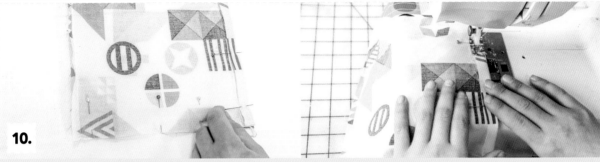

10.

Fold the piece in half with right sides together and pin. Placing the edge of the presser foot at the edge of the fabric and starting just under the second line of stitching, stitch down the side edge and across the bottom of the bag. Backstitch at the beginning and end.

11.

Trim the corners—but don't cut the stitching!

12.

Turn the bag right side out and press with an iron.

13.

Attach a small safety pin to the end of a length of twine at least 24″ long.

14.

Feed the safety pin through the little casing you created with the 2 lines of stitching. Go all the way through the casing and bring the pin out through the opening on the other side.

15.

Decide on the length of twine you want the finished bag to have and cut the ends even. Tie the ends together with a knot.

Once you know how to make this fun bag, start experimenting with different sizes. You could make a big wide one or maybe a tall skinny one … it's up to you!

Attach a sweet card and maybe a pom-pom or two and you are set!

Paper Flower Gift Toppers

Finished Size: Approximately 7″ in diameter

What Do I Need?

- Crepe paper in colors that would make a fun flower
- Scrap of felt measuring at least 3″ × 3″ for the flower base
- Hot glue gun (low temperature)
- Paper scissors

special skills

- Making and using templates (page 18)
- Using a hot glue gun (page 21)

Prepare the Pieces

1. Use the patterns (Paper Flower Topper, pages 132 and 133) to make templates.

2. Cut a stack of 6–8 of each different-sized petal from crepe paper.

3. Cut 1 strip for the inside of the flower from crepe paper.

4. Cut 1 felt circle.

TIP

Always cut the petals so that the grain (the lines in the crepe paper) is running up and down. This helps when it comes to shaping the petals.

Add a little taste of spring to your gift with this super-sweet paper flower gift topper. When the gift is opened, the flower could be sewn to a hair clip and worn in the recipient's hair ... how lovely!

125

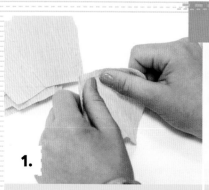

1.

Use your fingers to gently shape and stretch the petals so that they look a bit more like real flower petals.

2.

Starting around the outside edge of the felt circle, glue a couple of rows of overlapping large petals.

3.

Gradually start building the flower by adding rows of medium-sized petals inside the large petals.

4.

Next, fill in by adding rows of small petals.

5.

To make the inside of the flower, cut a fringe edge on the crepe paper strip.

6.

Roll up the fringe and secure with a bit of hot glue.

7.

Attach it to the center of the flower.

Felt Gift Card Holder

What Do I Need?

- 12″ × 12″ piece of felt
- Little fabric scraps
- Bright, fun-colored thread
- Fabric glue
- Pinking shears
- Perle cotton or embroidery floss
- Basic sewing supplies (page 10)

special skills

- Refer to The Rules of Sewing (page 7)
- Using an iron (page 19)
- Making and using templates (page 18)
- Sewing a running stitch (page 23)

Prepare the Pieces

1. Use the patterns (Felt Gift Card Envelope, Felt Gift Card Stamp, Felt Gift Card Address, Felt Gift Card Heart, pullout page P2) to make templates.

2. Trace the templates onto the appropriate fabrics.

3. Carefully cut out the shapes.

Let's Make It

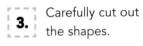

Thread the sewing machine with fun-colored thread and stitch around the entire envelope shape, sewing nice and close to the edge.

1.

127

Felt Gift Card Holder

I just love
giving gift cards ...
Sometimes they are
the perfect gift for
that person who has
everything!

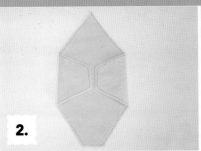

2.

Fold in the side flaps and press with an iron.

3.

Fold up the bottom flap and then the top flap and press with an iron.

4. Open it out and turn it over. The creases will help you work out where to place the stamp and address fabrics.

5. Use pinking shears to cut a fun edge around the stamp and the address fabric pieces.

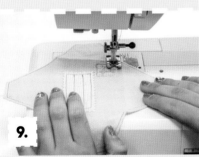

6.

Pin them in place wherever you like.

7.

Stitch around the address fabric, nice and close to the edge.

8.

Sew a couple of fun lines to add that address later.

9.

Sew around the stamp nice and close to the edge of the fabric.

10. & 11.

Refold the envelope and pin the lower flap to the side flaps.

Thread a needle with perle cotton or embroidery floss and use a simple running stitch to attach the lower flap to the sides.

12.

Apply a little fabric glue to the back of the heart and attach it to the middle of the upper envelope flap.

Kitty Catnip Toy

Cut 2 from felt.

Kitty Catnip Toy

Cut 8 from felt.

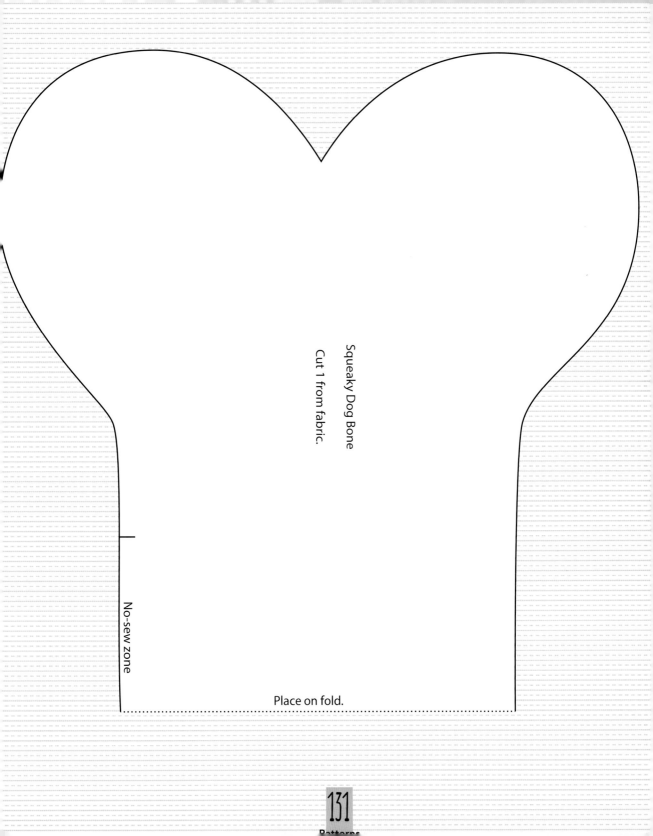

Squeaky Dog Bone

Cut 1 from fabric.

No-sew zone

Place on fold.

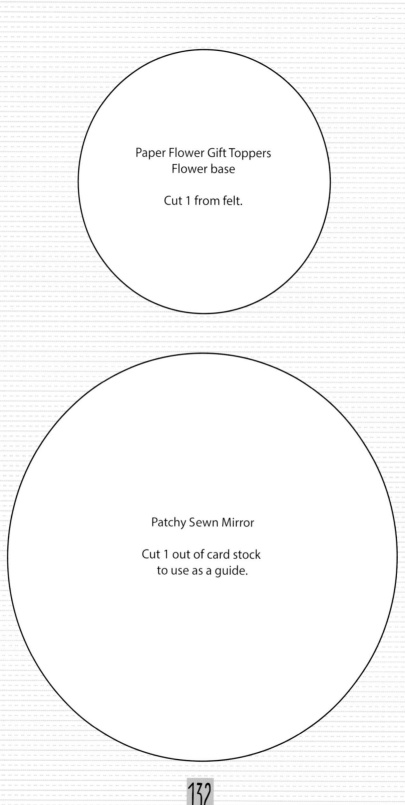

Paper Flower Gift Toppers
Flower base

Cut 1 from felt.

Patchy Sewn Mirror

Cut 1 out of card stock
to use as a guide.

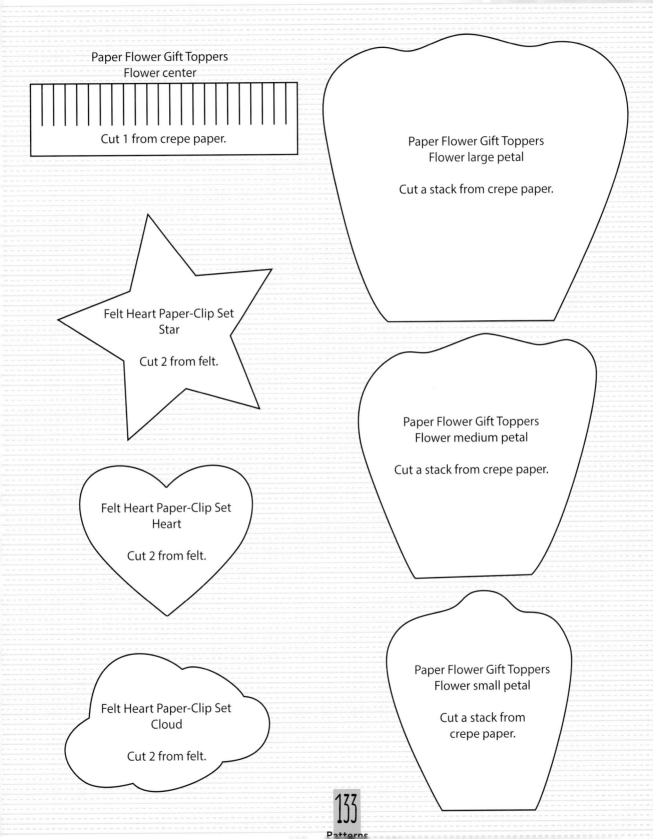

Paper Flower Gift Toppers
Flower center

Cut 1 from crepe paper.

Paper Flower Gift Toppers
Flower large petal

Cut a stack from crepe paper.

Felt Heart Paper-Clip Set
Star

Cut 2 from felt.

Paper Flower Gift Toppers
Flower medium petal

Cut a stack from crepe paper.

Felt Heart Paper-Clip Set
Heart

Cut 2 from felt.

Paper Flower Gift Toppers
Flower small petal

Cut a stack from
crepe paper.

Felt Heart Paper-Clip Set
Cloud

Cut 2 from felt.

Resources

My favorite shops and websites

Jo-Ann Fabric and Craft Stores
joann.com

Michael's Arts and Crafts
michaels.com

Fabric.com

Hawthorne Threads
hawthornethreads.com

Hancock fabrics
hancockfabrics.com

DMC (embroidery floss and perle cotton)
DMC.com

Paper Mart
papermart.com

134

About the Author

Annabel is a crafty Aussie mum and the owner of Little Pincushion Studio, a bright and fun sewing haven for many sweet and creative kids (littlepincushionstudio.com). She and her trusty sewing sidekick (and daughter) Ruby spend their afternoons teaching children everything they need to do to become confident sewing legends!

She writes a blog of the same name, where she shares her loves and inspirations in this creative world we live in.

Previous books by Annabel Wrigley:

FunStitch
✖ ✖ ✖ ✖ ✖ ✖ ✖ ✖ ✖
STUDIO

stitch your art out.

FunStitch Studio books are written and designed, specifically with kids, 'tweens and teens in mind!

"Every time I finish a project, **I get so excited**, because I feel like I can do **anything!**"
— Annalise, age 12

The text and projects are both age-appropriate and *nurture the love of handmade* in budding sewists, quilters, embroiderers and fashion designers.

by Judith Cressy

by Ali Benyon

by Brenna Maloney

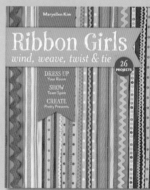

by Maryellen Kim

See the complete list of FunStitch Studio titles at ctpub.com/funstitch-studio/

FunStitch
STUDIO
an imprint of C&T Publishing